PRAISE FOR *EVOLVING*

"*Evolving While Black* is right on time. It is easy to relate to Chianti Lomax, as another highly credentialed Black woman with a similar Southern Baptist upbringing who was expected to excel and go above and beyond, while going along to get along and being all things to all people. I see a lot of myself in her stories, and her writing is so familiar that I know the practices she espouses are directly applicable. I will use her chapter on boundaries as my own personal guide. Seeing how the lack of boundary setting was controlling my life—from my emotional energy to time to physical resources—and learning how to set limits, even when others don't expect me to, is a defiant act of self-care. This is a must-read, and it actually 'read' me without even trying. Chianti is a friend we all want, with practical advice we need."

BÄRÍ A. WILLIAMS
startup adviser and former lead counsel at Facebook; author of *Seen Yet Unseen*

"As a Black woman who juggles a million things all the time, this book was a breath of fresh air. *Evolving While Black* not only helped me feel less selfish when tending to my own needs, but made me realize that we must do this for our self-preservation, survival, and sanity. Chianti Lomax uses examples from her life to connect while providing a road map through the feelings that may come when you confront your traumas, give yourself grace, and understand that loving yourself in daily bits of practice is the way to walking out a joyous and liberated life."

DEESHA DYER
former Obama White House social secretary; author of *Undiplomatic*

"Chianti Lomax gets it! She speaks directly to the heart of her reader. I found myself audibly saying YES many times. I appreciated reading a self-development book that accounts for how the complexities of race and gender can affect our mental health. Throughout the pages, I felt seen, acknowledged, and gently pushed toward more healing and transformation. This is an accessible and relatable guide for Black women on their healing journey while still being lighthearted and fun to read. Chianti provides useful strategies, relatable stories, and actionable steps to transform your life."

SHELAH MARIE
founder of Curvy, Curly, Conscious; author of *Unruly*

"Chianti Lomax has a distinctive ability to make the path toward personal breakthroughs and joy accessible to those seeking to propel their transformation. In *Evolving While Black*, she offers a clear framework that guides readers into understanding themselves, their mental barriers, and the tools and community they need to blossom in work and life. *Evolving While Black* is necessary and timely. At a time when it's harder than ever to sustain our mental well-being, this book is a resource for Black women to navigate their healing journeys, shift into mindfulness, and specify their needs in pursuit of happiness. Chianti's expertise as a transformational coach focuses on positive psychology, and her relatable and often humorous storytelling makes her a trusted voice that captivates readers from cover to cover."

CHLOE DULCE LOUVOUEZO
senior creative producer at the Bill & Melinda Gates
Foundation; author of *Life, I Swear*

EVOLVING WHILE BLACK

EVOLVING WHILE BLACK

The Ultimate Guide to
Happiness & Transformation
on Your Own Terms

CHIANTI LOMAX

sounds true
BOULDER, COLORADO

Sounds True
Boulder, CO

Published 2024

Cover and book design by Charli Barnes

Printed in the United States of America

BK06736

Library of Congress Cataloging-in-Publication Data

Names: Lomax, Chianti, author.
Title: Evolving while Black : the ultimate guide to happiness and transformation on your own terms / Chianti Lomax.
Description: Boulder, CO : Sounds True, 2024. | Includes bibliographical references.
Identifiers: LCCN 2023039866 (print) | LCCN 2023039867 (ebook) | ISBN 9781649631442 (trade paperback) | ISBN 9781649631459 (ebook)
Subjects: LCSH: African American women--Psychology. | African American women--Social conditions. | Change (Psychology) | Self-realization in women. | Happiness.
Classification: LCC E185.86 .L623 2024 (print) | LCC E185.86 (ebook) | DDC 155.8/496073--dc23/eng/20231106
LC record available at https://lccn.loc.gov/2023039866
LC ebook record available at https://lccn.loc.gov/2023039867

To my grandmothers . . .
may I continue to live out all your
wildest dreams

Love yourself at and in every evolution . . . Be proud of yourself for having the bravery to grow. Be proud of yourself for finding tools and figuring this sh*t out . . . Give yourself permission to evolve as often as you need to and any way that you need to without explanation.

Janelle Monáe[1]

CONTENTS

INTRODUCTION

Black people don't do stuff like this was the first thought that echoed in my mind as I looked at my Groupon receipt for a tandem skydiving jump. My second thought was, *I am not telling Ann Lomax about this until after my feet touch God's green earth.* And guess what? I did not!

Many years ago, I was sitting at work checking my personal email (y'all know some of us like to take a mental health break in the middle of a workday; it's called balance) and came across an email that would forever change my life. The email subject read, "Face Your Fears with This New Groupon Deal for Skydiving!" Face your fears? *Um, hello, Universe? Stay out of my business.* I'm a firm believer in God winks, and clearly there were some things that God knew I needed to sort out. So I decided to take the hint and purchase the deal, but not before I called my partner-in-foolishness, Tomara (also known as Tomkins), and convinced her to take the jump with me.

On a random Saturday morning in the fall, we made the drive down to a small airport in Warrenton, Virginia. We pulled up to the address from my Groupon and found two large barns, a medium-sized plane, and a tiny plane not too far from it.

As we signed in for our pre-jump training, Tomkins asked the receptionist, "Where is the plane we'll be jumping from today?"

The lady grinned and said, "Oh, that small one over there, sweetie."

Tomkins took one look at the plane, then looked at me and said, "Giiirrrl, I'll see you when you land."

Ma'am! I stood there in disbelief, but quickly got over it as it was my idea to jump out of a plane in the first place. I couldn't hold it against her. My mind, on the other hand, was made up. I didn't drive down those country roads for nothing! I walked up to the registration window, signed my name on the "If you die, it's not our fault" waiver, then introduced myself to my assigned tandem instructor—a tall, handsome man named Inan. He was a cool-looking man with dyed hair and an amazing accent—the perfect cheerleader, bursting with smiles and *tons* of energy while we waited for our jump time.

As we stood in our safety circle to receive our final pre-jump instructions, I glanced around and wondered why all these folks were here. What convinced them to jump out of a perfectly functioning airplane? I knew why I was there. I was tired. Tired of being afraid, tired of allowing other folks' perception of me to dictate my life, tired of letting fear and anxiety block me from taking risks, tired of doubting myself because of where I came from and what I was taught to believe about being Black in America. I was in mid-thought when I realized it was my group's turn to board the plane. To this day, I feel like Inan was the DJ Khaled to my big moment. With his handheld camera (because, yes, I paid the premium to get it all recorded) and *loud* words of affirmation, I felt like I could do anything.

"Let's GOOO!" he yelled as he made his way toward the plane. I quickly followed behind, feeling my adrenaline pumping. Surprisingly, I was more excited than afraid.

I walked past Tomkins, who nervously waved at me and said, "See you when you get back!" With eyes locked, we both said a silent prayer. This was it. My moment.

My group boarded the plane last and made our way to our seats. I counted from the front and realized Inan and I would be the fourth instructor-jumper pair. "Focus on your breath," I whispered to myself as we prepared for takeoff. The engine cranked on, and suddenly there was a choir of instructor-jumper conversations happening all at once. Inan gave me one last DJ Khaled pep talk.

"They didn't want us to jump. They didn't want us to risk it all. God DID!" OK, he didn't really say that, but the spirit of it was very similar.

Within a few minutes, my mind zoned out, and I started to pray. A wave of calmness fell over me as the airplane gained altitude. Instead of nervousness, I felt stillness, and my heartbeat slowed. It's hard to explain how at ease I felt in my heart and spirit. There were no feelings of fear or anxiety. I felt safe. I felt protected.

Suddenly, I was snapped out of my meditative state by a woman in front of me who began to weep hysterically. At that moment, I think she realized she was making a terrible decision. I mean, looking back years later, skydiving is a bit intense, so I can't even blame the lady for freaking out. Her instructor tried their best to calm her down because we had finally reached the jump zone and the only way down was by parachute. The door flew open, and everyone started to scoot toward the jumping position. The first tandem pair jumped, then the second, and then it was the weeping lady's turn, who, at this point, was screaming that she had made a mistake. Despite her initial protesting, her instructor managed to get her together just enough and began counting down to their jump: 5, 4, 3, 2, 1.

Then it was my turn. Inan scooted us toward the door. My mind was still fairly calm, but my heart was now beating out of my chest. Inan quickly reminded me of the jump instructions we learned on the ground, then said, "LEAN BACK!" WHOOOOOSH! We began to fall, and the sound of the wind rushing past my face was deafening. Finally, after what felt like a lifetime, my parachute opened, and the first words that dropped out of my lips as I caught my breath were "Thank you, Jesus!" followed by the infamous award-winning speech, "Mama, I made it!" For the next five minutes or so, we gracefully floated in the air. I was in awe. The one thought I had over and over again was *Wow, look at what God has done.* All the beauty was overwhelming. Miles and miles of lush greenery and fields. Gazing out into the horizon, for the very first time in my life, I felt clear, I felt open, I felt free. And even though my feet were as high as they'd ever been, I'd never felt more grounded.

We slowly lowered until I felt grass underneath me. I took a deep breath and felt so full of this new energy that I could feel my heart smiling. Goodness gracious! What was this newness that I felt down to the core of my being? I knew at that moment this newfound awareness would come with a price tag. It needed more space to grow and be cultivated so it could have a permanent home in my life. That jump was just the beginning of what would be years of jumping out of figurative planes and unlocking areas of myself that had been blocked by my chosen narratives, insecurities, and fears.

Speaking of fear, writing this freaking book might be my BIGGEST leap in my life to date. The overwhelm and imposter syndrome I had to overcome while pouring my soul into these pages—sheesh!

Before I even thought of jumping out of planes and getting my mental and emotional life together, I diligently worked as a management consultant. The first fifteen years of my professional consulting career was focused on organizational changes, which really shaped my trajectory as a business transformation consultant. To date, I have helped Fortune 500 companies and federal government agencies alike move through various types of change for their people, processes, technologies, or a combination of the three. My role during these large-scale projects would often focus on helping the people—the actual humans who were in the midst experiencing the organizational shift—navigate change. Starting with building an effective communications plan, I would gently guide them toward acceptance with human-focused training and empower them toward advocacy by creating sustainable systems.

If you've ever run a business or have been in a leadership role, then you know change in any organization is not for the faint of heart. I found myself working more of my coaching muscles as I navigated conversations around fear, job security, and early retirement. Those moments felt like a mental boot camp. I had federal government clients who were used to completing processes a certain way for over twenty years, and I was not only explaining how to operate a new software but also how their job role might change. If you could have only been a fly on those government classroom walls, then you would truly understand that I am a battle-tested coach and facilitator for any work environment.

I'm not going to lie—tapping into my emotional and social intelligence on a regular basis was a challenge, but it was also an energizing experience. Looking back at those client conversations, I realize that participating in this type of consulting work nurtured my passion for helping humans navigate the one thing that is constant in this life: change. My clients' breakthroughs and aha moments gave me a natural high, and as I progressed in my career, I was inspired to start my own lifestyle coaching business to help even more people. Everything I learned from my early consulting days at IBM, Accenture, and Deloitte, fused with my formal training as an executive coach and positive psychology practitioner, shapes how I help my current clients get results in their personal and professional growth.

In my late twenties and early thirties, I had a few moments where I thought, *What in the hell does any of this work have to do with my life's purpose? How is this work changing the world?* In those moments, I always referred back to my time in the OG Oprah hive, as she is someone who always stayed locked in on spreading the message of living out our life's purpose. As I navigated my early professional days, I heard her voice echo in my head at least once a year, lovingly shading me into being a productive citizen of the world. So, how was this work changing my world or the world of the people who look like me? Well, at the time, the easy answer was "Listen, you're getting a paycheck. Doesn't that count toward generational wealth?" That was valid, but my intuition kept telling me there was something greater.

Today, as a certified executive coach, it's easy for me to see how my work then and my approach to helping clients now are in alignment. Oprah would be so, so proud!

As I continued to grow professionally, I developed a healthy obsession with personal development and found joy in learning new ways to support myself and others through challenges and increase my understanding of how we're wired as humans. This infatuation with human development and growth is what drew me closer to positive psychology.

My introduction to the science of positive psychology came through a coaching program I enrolled in, and I immediately felt connected to its research and interventions. Martin Seligman, sometimes known as the father of positive psychology, describes it as "the scientific study of strengths that enables individuals and communities to thrive."[1] I know we just met, so you may not know this, but that definition has Chianti written all over it. Why? Let me put you onto some game. So, boom, traditional psychology (think: talk therapy) is based on a disease model, which focuses on simply remedying ailments. Positive psychology is like the 2.0 version of this, focusing instead on the wellness continuum, which asserts that you can use your strengths to improve your overall well-being. Some folks hear the name and assume it's all fluff, but positive psychology is not just about positive thinking or ignoring what's wrong. Instead, it's about developing a more balanced approach to growth and wholeness so you can live a fulfilled life on your own terms. This perspective is the wave I'm on.

By the end of my coaching certification program, I wanted to take a deeper dive into this new world I was exposed to. My plan was to apply to the University of Pennsylvania's Positive Psychology Center, where many of the elite positive psychology researchers had gotten their advanced degrees and were teaching. One of my coaching program advisors, and also a graduate of the Penn program, recommended I instead take an applied learning path that would save me both time and money (and your girl loves to save a coin).

Soon, I found myself sitting in my applied positive psychology program, and that's when I realized there was a personal trend happening at the end of each day. Our professor would lecture, we would pair up with a classmate to practice an intervention or method, and I would often end up in tears, y'all. Like real tears. Happy tears. Healing tears. Reflective tears. I would be damn near dehydrated after a full day of class. At some point, I even stopped wearing mascara to class. I mean, the water works flowed freely. At the end of each session, I couldn't help but think, *Man, if only I'd learned this as a child.* And sometimes I would turn to the only other woman of color and whisper, "Black and brown people need this," and she would give me a head tilt with pursed lips that said, "For real, though."

By the time we reached graduation, a true internal shift had taken place. Curiosity and healing started to replace my fears, doubts, and shame. I now had language and tools to make sense of my own humanity, and my happiness and well-being felt a bit more sacred. I realized that, for years, I'd been resting in a mindset of lack and relinquishing my power to my past. During my time in that program, I was able to make peace with the dynamic nature of my thoughts and emotions and learn how to acknowledge them without losing my agency. And in understanding more about myself and how I'm wired, I even learned to have a little more empathy and patience with family and friends. When I began to look at the inner child within myself and the people around me, I was able to reevaluate my expectations and biases, creating the space to improve and mend many of my relationships—most importantly, the one I had with myself.

From a personal and professional perspective, I'd found the jackpot of personal growth resources. Regardless of how amazingly helpful I found the information to be, there was still one glaring observation that I couldn't help but notice with every new book, research article, or TED Talk I came across in the positive psychology space: none of the authors, speakers, or researchers looked like me, and I took that personally. To many of us personal development connoisseurs, it might feel like there is limitless access to research-based information on self-improvement, transformation, and positive thinking; however, the fact remains that there is a large segment of people who look like *us* and don't bother to pick up these resources, usually for one of two reasons: one, the message is too jargon-heavy, dry, or boring, so the jewels get lost in translation, or two, they can't connect to the *messenger*. And rightfully so, right? I mean, not too many of us in the "rooting for everybody Black" era are going to take life advice from a seventy-five-year-old white man. Trust issues with white male patriarchy is a real thing. And can you blame us? I know I cannot speak for every Black person's experience because Black people are not a monolith, but I am indeed rooting for peace, growth, and happiness for the entire diaspora, which is why I wrote this book.

I might be jumping the shark here, but I am confident that, while reading this book, you will find at least one powerful nugget that will be a catalyst for change in your life, big or small. And hey, guess what? A win is a win. My hope is that you revisit this book anytime you're in need of a re-up on a little happiness and a lot of healing. Everything you'll uncover in these pages is inspired by the science of flourishing and well-being, which can best be outlined through the PERMA model. PERMA stands for Positivity, Engagement, Relationships, Meaning, and Achievement, and it's like a cheat code for improving your overall well-being while minimizing factors that might cause you stress. I frequently sprinkle PERMA all up and through my personal coaching, so I've decided to do the same for this book, using its building blocks the same way most Black folks use laundry detergent: like seasoning.

If you've picked up this book, there are few things that might be taking place in your world. Let's start with the fact that you understand there is a divine assignment placed over your life, but you may be overwhelmed and, dare I say, exhausted from all the responsibility that lands on your plate. You have big, audacious dreams that require a version of you that feels out of reach, mainly because limiting beliefs and self-doubt have camped out in your mental space. You desire to break free, but procrastination and people pleasing have you in a chokehold. The growth and progress you desire has not been able to take root because your life is filled with thoughts and behaviors that are serving as barriers to the life you deserve. Or maybe you're just social media coached out. You've watched so many reels and saved so many life advice graphics, but none of it is sticking to your bones. I see you, I feel you, and I understand you. I've been there. I've been in a place where I was on the brink of a shift, but I lacked the direction and support needed to turn that corner. My hope for you is that by the time you reach the end of this book, your load will feel a little lighter. I hope you gain the courage and confidence to unsubscribe from any part of your life that has been holding your greatest self hostage. You will have the boundaries and belief systems required to finally be the version of you who is ready to be set free.

So listen, the Type A side of my personality loves an outline and a plan, so to honor her, let's briefly get into our phased approach as we move forward in this book together.

Phase 1: We're going to **get curious with care**. In order to do this, we'll need to build self-awareness around limiting beliefs, outdated belief systems, and unhealthy habits. Bag lady, get ready to let it go because we will be doing a *ton* of unpacking. My goal is to help you identify what might not be the most helpful or healthy. I'm not going to lie to you; this might cause a rush of emotions, insecurities, and maybe even a little anxiety. But understand that I got you, and most importantly, *you* got you. Extend yourself some grace and compassion during this phase because, truth be told, up until this point, you've been doing the best you can with what you were given.

Phase 2: You're going to **break up with your blockers**. Once you've become aware of your unhealthy thoughts, habits, and behaviors, it's time to do something about them. Identifying unhealthy mindsets and behaviors is only half the battle. This part of the journey is where I start to introduce tools for self-care, healing, and mass construction so you can build and broaden along the way.

Phase 3: Finally, we're going to **cultivate a community** for your insights and growth. How? With built-in accountability. We will close out this book by making sure you have a built-in support system for the journey ahead. Growth is never a straight line. You'll grow. You'll backpedal. You'll learn, and then you'll grow some more. Think of the resources in this phase as bread crumbs that will help you find your way back on track if you fall off or lose sight of the vision. The secret weapon to your progress in this phase will be surrounding yourself with people and primers (more on this later) that can help you honor the highest version of yourself.

Tall order, right? Perhaps, but you've got this. Together, we will focus on ways to support your growth with grace. Just think of me as the DJ Khaled to your personal evolution. After each breakthrough, we'll tackle *another one* and then *another one*! Now if you're not a DJ Khaled fan, instead think of me as an honest bestie that reminds you of your inner beauty and holds you accountable for protecting it. Use this book to help you unpack what weighs you down, heal the things holding you hostage, and get back to the refreshing and rewarding parts of life. My hope is that this book provides you with a life-altering experience, an experience that is so dope and mind-blowing that you revisit certain chapters once or twice a year just to make sure the growth is secured.

The world is in shambles, and I don't foresee it never not being in shambles. However, I'm on a mission to make sure Black people never give up on creating their own little corners of healing and happiness, as this is a rebellious act against racism and patriarchy. This is what drives my passion for supporting you as you uncover the highest version of yourself. With each level of growth, you will unlock hidden superpowers to inspire yourself and support generations of Black women and children who come after you. As I said earlier, I recognize that Black women and black folks, in general, are not monolithic. Throughout this book, I am speaking from my own unique experience, and my intention is for you walk away from our time together with practical tools and universal truths to design a life that allows YOU to be the most fully expressed version of yourself.

Before you start tiptoeing through these pages, I recommend that you dedicate a journal, tablet, or mobile device to record your thoughts, reactions, annoyances, or insights. I say this with love and a side of accountability: put this book down and go grab something. Please and thank you.

In terms of who all gon' be there? Right now, it's just me, you, an ounce of courage, a drop of openness, and your journal. Are you ready? Let's get started.

CHAPTER 1

SELF-AWARE AF

You Gotta Know the Root to Get to the Fruit

hink warm thoughts, think warm thoughts. Jesus, be a pair of long johns and a heated blanket, I thought. It was January 21, 2012, as I stood in a sea of faces at the United States Capitol, waiting for our forever First Lady Michelle Obama and her husband President Barack Obama to accept another term in the good ole White House. I promise you it felt like one of the coldest days of my life. I just knew I was going to freeze a few two-strand twists off that day. Despite it being disrespectfully cold, I remember standing there in awe. That was my second time attending an inauguration for President Obama, but I still got a little choked up thinking about the monumental occasion. Our first Black president was getting sworn in for the second time. Man, what a time to be alive, and I was grateful just to be in that number.

I moved to Washington, DC (a.k.a. the DMV), at a pivotal moment in my adult life. I was exploring womanhood outside of my mom and childhood friends, and being out and about in the nation's capital allowed me the privilege to meet many influential people who looked like me, from political figures and civil rights heroes to CEOs, venture capitalists, spiritual leaders, and even Black Arts Movement icons. The abundance of Black excellence was overwhelming at times, and I was constantly reminded that I was a long way from Greenville, South Carolina. Even going to church was different in the DMV.

I remember getting a phone call from one of my close friends one Easter Sunday, giving me the heads-up that I should come super early to church that day. Even though I always arrive early to get a good parking space and a good seat toward the front of the congregation, this Sunday was different. I walked up to the front of the church and saw huge metal detectors at the entrances with secret service officers lining the perimeter of the building. Guess who'd decided to join us for church service that morning? Auntie Michelle, her husband Barack, and our White House cousins, Sasha and Malia.

If you're from a major city, then you're probably thinking, *So what? I see successful Black people of this caliber all the time.* That is wonderful, and you've had a very blessed life. You hang tight for a second while I talk to my small-town cousins who understand me. Growing up in South Carolina, I didn't see many models of local successful Black folks. For many Black people in my hometown, securing a job at the local factory on the outskirts of the city was considered a high-paying job, and if you were lucky, you might have found your way into education as a teacher. On my side of the tracks, job opportunities for people who looked like me were either in manual labor, education, or the beauty industry. Please don't misunderstand me—those options provide an honest and decent life, but something in me knew there had to be more.

I was raised by a single-parent in a working-class home with my mom and three siblings. We didn't grow up with a lot of material things, but my mother was one of the most resourceful and creative women I've ever known. Although she instilled key values in me, such as independence, resilience, faith, and assertiveness, she couldn't protect me from the harsh realities I would face growing up as a Black girl in the South. Of course, there was no comparison to what our parents and grandparents went through as children, but racism was still there, parading around as redlining, forced busing, and tracking in our school systems.

As a little Black girl living in the Bible Belt, I inadvertently adopted beliefs on how I would be perceived in a predominantly white school, how I should act and behave as opposed to my white classmates, and the many limitations society would try to place on me as a double minority. I was often told that *they* didn't want me to be *too* successful because of the color of my skin. Talk about deflating. Unfortunately, this is a norm in many Black households in America, especially in the South. If I'm being honest, the idea of *they* sounded like the boogeyman in a scary movie that would follow me at every turn and watch my every move. *They* didn't want me to grow up and thrive. *They* didn't want me to learn about our real history in schools. *They* didn't want me to eat seasoned chicken. Too far? I know. But you know exactly what I mean.

At an early age, I knew people who looked like me faced real-life threats because of systemic racism and learned bigotry. At the same time, I understood that the racism I would bump into might look a little different from colored-only bathrooms or policemen's water hoses. I soon found out that it would show up in my relationships with predominantly white teachers, my interactions with salesclerks at expensive stores, or even sharing the sidewalks of Charleston, South Carolina, with people who "didn't see me" as we passed each other. This is so disgusting to think about in this day and age, but it is still our reality, and we all know that having *the talk* with our parents or grandparents is just one of our unfortunate rites of passage as a Black child.

Let's make one thing clear, though. What we're not about to do is subscribe to hopelessness around here. I rebuke the "woe is me" way of thinking in the name of Black Jesus. There are many examples of our Black brothers and sisters who have beaten the odds, and I've decided to join them in the history books (or on *Black Enterprise*, *The Breakfast Club*, or the OWN Network). I am inspired by the great negro spiritual "We Gone Make It" by the legendary Psalmist Jadakiss. And here I am today, still keeping it moving. You can call it naivety or blame it on my early obsession with hip-hop, but in my mind, I've always felt I was destined for an "It was all a dream" Biggie moment.

When I heard retired NFL legend and *The Pivot Podcast* host Fred Taylor say, "Exposure leads to expansion," it felt like a nod to my inner child. This statement is so simple but so profound, and its essence has been a foundational pillar in how I've navigated life. By the time I got to high school, I had already set my sights on leaving the state of South Carolina. I didn't know where I would land, but the one thing I did know was that I would be closer to my dreams—and that's word to Goapele.

I want you to view growth seasons, no matter what your circumstances may look like, in the same way. You might not understand how you're going to get to the other side of your troubles, but lean on the old Black adage of *where there is a will, there is a way*. The first destination on this journey starts by traveling within. For transformation to take place, you must understand where you are in order to get a clear perspective of where you need to go. The *Oxford Dictionary* defines the word *transformation* with phrases such as "a dramatic change in form" or "a metamorphosis." But what I've learned from years of helping leaders move their workforces through tech transformations is that it's vital to start with understanding the current state. When I support my coaching clients who feel stuck, we start with their current state. I guide them through self-awareness practices that uncover their current beliefs, behaviors, and energy gains and drains. We then take time to break all of these unpacked personal details into five areas of well-being: career, financial, health, social, and community. Of course, these areas aren't 100 percent inclusive; however, they represent the things researchers typically deem as essential to living a full life. Let's take a moment to break these down real quick.

Career well-being is all about how you occupy your time and how much you enjoy what you do every single day. This one is so important because we spend most of our time each day working at a job or vocation. You don't have to be balling out of control for your career well-being to be flourishing; all that matters is that you are engaged in something you actually like doing. Let's take our girl Synclaire, for example. Synclaire's parents wanted her to follow the family's tradition of graduating from Morgan State and becoming a teacher, but after college, she decided to move to LA to pursue singing full-time. Even though she is singing background for a major artist and it's light-years away from what her family wants, it fills her with joy to use her voice to bring smiles to the audience members' faces every single night.

Similarly, **financial well-being** has nothing to do with the amount of money you have, but has everything to do with being a good steward of your coins by living within or below your means as opposed to sitting under mountains of debt. For example, Max is an HR professional and part-time makeup artist who makes $85,000 a year and consistently contributes to her retirement fund. She doesn't play about keeping her debt at bay, outside of student loans; she keeps all of her credit card balances paid off. Max even has enough coins saved up for a rainy day and to take an international vacation at least once a year. Now, Max is not a millionaire by any stretch of the imagination, but she's smart with her cash, and is able to use it wisely to live a comfortable life.

Social well-being relates to your ability to have meaningful, strong relationships and love in your life. Reliable, positive relationships can help you live longer, reduce stress, and boost your immune system. Khadijah is a perfect example of what high social well-being looks like, as she lives with her cousin and one of her besties in New York City. As a household, their social rituals include daily roommate breakfasts at the kitchen table and a weekly life talk session on Wednesdays over wine and wings. Now that many of her friends are married with children, she hosts a game night once a month to stay connected while catering to their new responsibilities. She maintains a close relationship with her new boo, Terrence, whom she has been seeing exclusively for nine months. Her life is filled with both platonic and romantic love.

Physical well-being is about making good health decisions and setting positive habits that allow you to function optimally. It's not about having perfect health. This kind of well-being focuses on things like improving your sleep, developing a balanced diet, deep breathing exercises for relaxation, gentle stretching, performing activities in ways that curate a sense joy in your body, and having enough energy to do what needs to be done each day. Regine is really killing it in this area. She drinks her water, takes her vitamins, and only has her favorite fried foods once a month. She makes sure she gets at least seven to eight hours of sleep every night, and she religiously takes daily walks around her neighborhood before she starts her workday.

The last area, **community well-being**, relates to how much you engage with your neighbors and immediate environment and recognize that you are part of something bigger than yourself. I typically tie in faith and spirituality here, as these aspects of life usually involve those in our community. Brother William has his community well-being on lock. He has recently moved to an affluent Black county that caters to the Black boy joy that lives inside of him. His neighbors are retired federal government workers who grab his packages and mail for him when he goes out of town, he attends meditation sessions at the local community center twice a week, and he recently joined two of his church's ministries so he can use his gifts for good. To top it all off, he often visits a local Black-owned coffee shop that is a frequent pit stop for local Black politicians and community organizers.

Segmenting your life into areas of well-being is an easy way to create a baseline for how you define your quality of life. Let's say you're running a little low on gas in one of the five areas because, well, life. All is not lost because guess what? You can do the work to improve it. Since no one human being is the same, there are many ways to do this, but your goal is to discover what works for you to improve the quality of your life. These areas of well-being are interdependent. If you go through a season where you're not getting enough sleep on a regular basis, you're eating tons of unhealthy foods, and Tequila Tuesdays have turned into Tequila Everydays, you might start noticing a change in other areas of your life. For example, the energy and focus you once had at work or in your volunteer events might turn into exhaustion, lack of motivation, and interest. When you are intentional about strengthening your overall well-being, focusing on one area at a time, your life will start to feel way more balanced and manageable. I'm a living witness that this is true!

CHAPTER CHECK-IN

The Invitation: Find a quiet place where you won't be disturbed. In your journal, check in on your own quality of life and where it stands right now. Rate your areas of well-being from one to ten, with ten being "I'm killing it in this area" and one being "Put it in rice. I need a do-over." Jump right in and do not overthink your responses. There's no one peeking over your shoulder to judge you. It might help to set a three- to five-minute timer to discourage overthinking, but this is not mandatory.

Honestly assess where you are in each area of well-being and add up the scores. Did any areas surprise you? If you scored any of the areas seven and below, put a star by it and write out what you could do to eventually make it a ten. If you can't think of anything at the moment, that's okay. Embrace the unknown and keep on trucking.

Congratulations, you have just taken your first step toward increasing your self-awareness!

SELF-AWARENESS

To ensure we're operating from the same level of understanding as we begin to increase our self-awareness, let's define it as the ability to see your strengths and weaknesses honestly, clearly, and objectively, and to consciously understand how they influence your actions and interactions with other people. Great, so how do we achieve self-awareness? Through intentional self-reflection and introspection. As we go through and grow through changes in our lives, it's important to take time to regularly look back on what we've been through, good and bad. Have you ever heard of beer goggles? Well, limited or low self-awareness works in the same way, clouding our ability to see a situation for what it is. Self-awareness helps us take off these villain goggles we typically put on subconsciously after a disagreement or unfavorable experience. It's so much easier to escape accountability and find the villain in every scenario when you have your goggles on. But it takes true awareness to be able to honestly face where you are going wrong and what needs to be done to remedy the situation. I often ask myself: What am I holding onto that I need to let go of? What could I do differently in the future? What is it that I really want from the people I care about? The goal here is not to get stuck in rumination or self-pity, but to reflect with the intention of uncovering insights and growth opportunities.

Think of self-awareness the same way you think about getting in shape physically. The more you exercise, the better you get at it; and the more you practice focusing on your well-being areas, the greater your awareness will become. My clients love getting practice with the well-being areas, as it helps them take a step back and get curious about their life as a whole. It puts them in the observer seat without it feeling like a chore so they can lean into self-discovery, which is the basis of my coaching practice. Oftentimes, I take on the role of co-pilot for my clients, guiding and supporting them through what they're learning on their own. I'd rather they uncover what's happening internally so the lessons can stick. So think of the well-being check-in as your pre-workout assessment, and as a member of your personal training team, I now know your starting point.

Research by the Eurich Group reveals that even though most people think they are hyper-aware of their strengths and weaknesses, only about 10 to 15 percent of the 5,000 people they studied actually met the criteria set forth to denote higher levels of self-awareness.[1] Check this out: the research also concluded that having objective clarity on your values, thoughts, feelings, strengths, and weaknesses allows us to feel more in control of our lives, maintain meaningful relationships, and experience higher career satisfaction. In other words, you can literally become the hero in your own story and maybe even those of the people you love most.

If that isn't a good enough reason to consider working on your self-awareness, then maybe these additional benefits will convince you.

Benefits of High Self-Awareness

- **Higher creativity:** Knowing who you are enhances your ability to generate new ideas and think outside the box. This helps with problem-solving and finding more value at work (or in business).

- **Regulated emotions:** When negative emotions arise, you'll be more equipped to identify what they are and what's causing them, then manage your responses accordingly. Believe or not, this will help you keep your stress levels at bay.

- **Wiser decision-making:** You tend to move better and make smarter choices when you know who you are and aren't blinded by your biases and perceived limitations.

- **Stronger interpersonal connections:** Self-awareness not only improves your communication skills, but it also gives you space to cultivate empathy for those around you. As you learn more about who you are, you'll be able to better understand others' emotions and perspectives, which helps foster deeper relationships.

Now that you have a working definition of what self-awareness is and why it's vital in transforming your relationships and how you show up in the world, let's take this one level deeper.

As the Eurich Group continued to dig into their research, they came to the conclusion that people typically experience two types of self-awareness. They coined the first type as *internal self-awareness*, which is the examination of your stuff—you know, the things we mentioned earlier like thoughts, feelings, values, aspirations, and impact on others. The second was deemed *external self-awareness*, which is how others perceive our actions, values, and aspirations. Their research included surveying and conducting in-depth interviews across many countries while exploring the relationship between self-awareness and key attitudes and behaviors, like happiness, stress, job satisfaction, and empathy. The results showed that when you're aware of how other people perceive you, you're typically more skilled at displaying empathy toward others. Both types are equally important and should be given the same amount of attention and energy on your self-awareness journey.

At this point you're probably thinking, *OK, I know what self-awareness means, I know why it's important for me to thrive, and I even know the two types, but what does it look like when it's unhealthy? How do I know when my self-awareness meter is running low?* Let's walk through a few signs of a lack of self-awareness and how these unchecked signs might impact your quality of life.

Signs of Low Self-Awareness

- **Impulsivity:** Being impulsive signals that you might have an issue with self-regulation. This could show up as overreacting, overspending, overeating, or not thinking before acting. Any of these could damage your relationships, cause conflict, and/or affect your overall well-being.

- **Defensiveness:** When people in your life share feedback with you, you receive it as an attack rather than helpful constructive criticism and it's hard for you to accept fault or blame. This can create barriers to communication and understanding in your relationships.

- **Apathy:** You have a hard time understanding the experiences and feelings of other people and seeing other people's perspectives. This could manifest as a lack of concern and conflict in your personal and work life.

- **Excessive nostalgia:** It's hard for you to move on or get over things easily. You often find yourself ruminating on what could have been or what should have been. You believe focusing on the past gives you a sense of control, but it actually causes anxiety, guilt, and regret.

Whew! Do any of those resonate with you? I know I had to sweep around my own front door after that list. Be gentle with yourself when you acknowledge these hard truths. Self-awareness is not a destination; you have to keep doing the work to stay tuned in.

So, now you may be thinking, *Sis, how do I unlock this self-awareness thing you're talking about and stay tuned in?* First, relax your forehead!

Since being introduced to the concept of self-awareness as a coach, I've decided to simply integrate it into my daily routine, just like brushing my teeth or moisturizing my edges. Here are a few awareness hacks that will boost your self-awareness game to the next level. Go grab a pen and paper or open the Notes app on your phone and try one of these pro tips in your daily routine.

Pro Tips for Self-Awareness

- **Take a strengths assessment:** Strength assessments can be game changers to self-mastery. Knowing your strengths gives you more confidence to cope, problem solve, and create meaning in your life. My two faves to use with my coaching clients are the VIA Character Strengths Survey[2] by the VIA Institute of Character (this one is FREE dollars) or CliftonStrengths Assessment[3] by Gallup.

- **Visualize your ideal self:** Find a quiet place and answer the following questions to increase your success in overcoming obstacles and setbacks:

  ° Imagine yourself a year from now living your dream life.

  ° What does this ideal self look like?

  ° How does it feel to be this person?

  ° What values and qualities do you embody in this space?

- **Ask for feedback:** External feedback is just as important as internal feedback. External feedback helps you to identify your blind spots. Sometimes the people closest to you are able to see certain skills and characteristics that you ignore or just don't consider. They can also help you to see opportunities for growth that you're not aware of because they are on the receiving end of these behaviors and habits. Poll your friends, family, or colleagues for their input on your strengths and weaknesses. Ask them for written or verbal feedback depending on how you want to use it.

- **Commit to daily check-ins:** Daily check-ins help you to track your growth journey. When you are spending this dedicated time taking a close look at how your day went, it creates built-in accountability, increases your confidence in your own abilities, and can even boost your self-esteem. You're able to see in real time how things are progressing or how things might be receding. With this personal insight, you're equipped to make adjustments as needed on a day-to-day basis. Set aside a few minutes at the end of each day to check in with yourself. You can use a journal or the Notes app on your phone to capture what went well, what didn't go well, and what you want to do better the next day.

- **Write morning pages:** This pro tip is courtesy of Julia Cameron's *The Artist's Way*. I've found this practice to be super beneficial during those seasons when there are tons of moving pieces and my thoughts are going 100 mph. Not only does this practice help you tame your anxiety, it also helps you clear your mind so that you can have a more calm and mindful start to your day. Every morning, before you get out of bed, grab your journal and write out three full pages of your thoughts. Yes, three *full* pages. Allow your thoughts to flow freely, without judging them or expecting them to sound a certain way, and don't focus on grammar, spelling, or punctuation. Just keep writing what comes to mind. Also try not to re-read anything you've written until you're completely done. **This is a fan favorite with my friends and clients!**

All right, as we wrap up this chapter, let's do a quick rundown of what we've learned: Self-awareness is a foundational step in transforming and flourishing from the inside out. You can't flourish if you don't know who you are. And knowing yourself doesn't just benefit you; it influences and impacts those around you, as you'll foster more empathy for others, feel more confident and capable within yourself, and build deeper and more meaningful connections with the people you love. We love to see it!

CHAPTER CHALLENGE

Now I know you didn't think you were going to move on from this chapter without some meaningful homework to test-drive this goodness we just learned. Remember, building self-awareness takes practice, so it's important you work on this mental muscle as much as possible. There are two parts to this exercise to address the two categories of self-awareness: internal and external. Yay! If you're side-eyeing me right now, no worries! After completing this exercise, you're going to want to give me a big ole gratitude hug. OK, so boom, here is how this is going to work.

Part 1:
Morning Pages The Remix (Internal Self-Awareness)

The Invitation: I invite you to carve out time in your morning routine to complete five days of morning pages, but this is *Evolving While Black*, so you know I gotta remix it!

1. Go to your streaming service of choice and choose a playlist of songs that will help you create a nice, calm vibe. Need a little help? You can borrow mine until you have time to create your own by scanning this QR code.

2. Find a cozy, quiet place in your home that allows you to be alone.

3. Open a new note on your phone or find a clean page in your journal if you're a paper and pen kinda girl like me.

4. Now that the vibe is set, complete three pages of stream-of-consciousness writing. That's it. Just three pages. Write anything. Write everything. Write the word *the* fifty times in a row. Write whatever comes to your mind without censoring it.

5. Set an alarm on your phone so you can complete this at the same time every day.

For bonus points: You can make this experience extra vibey by lighting your favorite nontoxic scented candle or spraying your space with lavender. You'll thank me later.

> **GROW TIP:** If you're using a device of any kind to write, put it on airplane mode. This helps to minimize the distractions.

Part 2:
Poll Your Clique (External Self-Awareness)

The Invitation: Reach out to your friends, family, or colleagues for input on your strengths and opportunities (a.k.a. your weaknesses). I recommend you pick up the phone to call them or shoot them a text message for this exercise. Most of my friends have hectic schedules because of kids, spouses, and careers so I like to send voice messages or text messages. And to alleviate any pressure on them, I tell them they can reply through voice message or text message.

Suggested Questions to Ask: These are simply recommendations. Please feel free to tweak them to your liking.

- What would you say I'm really good at? List whatever comes to mind.

- What would you say are my real talents?

- What do you think is holding me back?

CHAPTER 2

IN THOSE GENES

The Truth about Happiness

In the last chapter, we tapped into the power of self-awareness and talked about how it gives us insight into who we are and how we relate to other people. By being in tune with our thoughts, emotions, and values, we can identify what really makes us happy and take the right steps to create more of it in our lives. Since you're all warmed up now, join me in exploring the science and truth about happiness and what role it plays on this journey of self-discovery.

CHAPTER CHECK-IN

Before we get into the juicy stuff surrounding happiness, let's do a proactive chapter check-in on your current relationship to happiness. We'll dive deeper as we move through this chapter, but it's important that you get a lay of the land before exerting any effort in learning and applying these concepts.

The Invitation: Grab your recording device of choice (your phone's Voice Memo app should do the trick) and set a timer. (I typically set mine for five minutes.) Take three deep breaths to center yourself in the present moment, inhaling through your nose and exhaling out your mouth.

Then, in the allotted time, answer the following prompts. If it takes you more time than what you originally allotted, feel free to keep talking.

- What words or thoughts come to mind when you hear the word *happiness*?

- What did happiness look like for you as a child?

- How has your view on happiness changed as an adult?

When you're finished answering these questions, take notice of your energy. Is it lighter or heavier than when you started the check-in? Remember, there is no judgment here; simply observe and keep a mental note of how you feel. All right? Good.

> **GROW TIP:** Put your phone on Do Not Disturb or silent to eliminate distractions.

"Come on, Derrick!" I said, picking up my little sister while my oldest brother grabbed our little brother out of his bed. It was time for our weekly childhood ritual to commence: wake up early on Saturday morning, gather the troops and a large blanket, make a few bowls of cereal, and sit on the couch to watch Saturday morning cartoons as a group. When I think about my happiest moments growing up, Saturday morning cartoons were top tier, Grammy Award-winning happiness. No frills. No gimmicks. Just me, my siblings, and a few good episodes of *Bobby's World*.

Admittedly, this kind of happiness is simple, but it's still valid. I've found in my work as a coach that when folks hear the word *happiness*, they immediately imagine unicorns, rainbows, sunny days, and Prince (or Princess) Charming coming to whisk them away from all their problems. Although, I love a good ol' problematic Disney Princess movie, that's not what I mean when I talk about happiness. When I teach women how to achieve happiness on their own terms, it's really focused on helping them navigate their daily responsibilities with a little more resilience. The glass slippers and prince are sold separately.

As a child, happiness felt way less complicated, but the older we get, the more complex our view of happiness becomes. Before I jump into what happiness *really* is, I'd like to tell you what it is not. Regardless of what your favorite social media influencer does or says, happiness is not about having a perfectly curated feed. Your life does not have to be picture-perfect for you to experience it. Happiness is not a destination you can reach; instead, it's more like an active journey of delightful and favorable experiences. Happiness is not about avoiding depression, stress, or any negative emotion, as this is not realistic. Instead, it is experiencing joy, fulfillment, and purpose, despite the heaviness of the world. I believe that happiness is not something that just happens to us, nor is it something to chase down. It is an intentional decision.

Once you understand that happiness is active and not passive, you can lean on your internal and external resources to call in more positive experiences, cope in healthier ways, and remain vigilant in the face of adversity. The lessons we learned on self-awareness in the last chapter will help you identify what brings you positive energy and joy so you can call more of that into your life on a consistent basis.

In 2016, 771 everyday working professionals were asked, "If you could say in one word what you want more of in life, what would that be?" The number one answer (yes, even ranking above money) was *happiness*. Kathy Caprino, senior *Forbes* contributor and therapist, went a step further to share that many of the professional women she worked with had a hard time putting a ring on happiness. Apparently, happiness is out here in these streets, trying its best to not get tied down. But when Caprino dug a bit deeper into why these women felt like they had so much trouble securing happiness in their lives, she found two main culprits: lack of self-awareness and a search for happiness in external things, such as a man, a career, or shopping.[1]

You might be thinking, *Wait a minute, now! My dark olive Telfar bag brings me tons of happiness*, and you're probably right! But the gems you need to catch from Caprino is this: if you continue subscribing to the idea that happiness is found outside of yourself, you're going to need a lot of water and a good pair of Hokas because, *chile'*, you will be chasing it for the rest of your life.

While we're on this topic, let me say this: I believe that happiness gets a bad rep.

After all, many people won't even admit that their main focus in life is happiness. They believe that monetary, social, or career success will eventually lead to it, refusing to care about or even acknowledge the importance of focusing on happiness itself. Well, as we've just learned, chasing happiness in outside things and situations is a recipe for disaster, but luckily for us, research backed by positive psychology heroes Sonja Lybumirsky, Ed Diener, and Laura King shared several reasons why intentional focus on happiness could grant you everything external and then some. I suggest you grab a highlighter or your recording device (if you're listening to the audiobook). You're going to want to save these gems for later.

WHY HAPPINESS MATTERS

- Happy people make more *schmoney* and are typically more productive at work.

- Happy people are generally in better health, get sick less often, and tend to live longer.

- Happy people are more likely to have fulfilling marriages, relationships, and friendships. (All the single ladies, all the . . . Too old of a reference? OK, that's fine. Let's move on.)

- Happy people are more charitable.

- Happy people cope better with stress and trauma.

- Happy people are more creative and are better able to see the big picture.

Happiness is a very personal and multifaceted concept, so what works for Brandy might not work for Monica, but you shouldn't underestimate the impact it can have on your road to transformation. Even with this level of subjectivity, there are concrete misconceptions that can block us from experiencing happiness in our own authentic way.

Speaking from personal experience and from my time coaching high-achieving Black women, many of us (especially women) have adopted warped views of "happily ever after." We're not 100 percent at fault for the fairy tales and fallacies we've adopted about happiness over the years. Much of our perspectives were fueled by messaging fed to us as little girls. We got it from all sides—our television shows, movies, toys, and even books. Those early 2000s rom-coms had us believing we should all marry a super wealthy man who will rescue us from our mundane lives, or that life really begins when we marry the man of our dreams. And let's not even stop at childhood; now we've been gifted with social media feeds filled with #CoupleGoals, #BodyInspo, or #BossBabe imagery. Although the intention most times is to be inspirational, I've found that it's been more harmful to my clients' confidence and self-awareness than anything else. In fact, let me share three common happiness misconceptions that might be blocking you from enjoying a meaningful, happy life right now.

- **I'll be happy once I start my business or find my dream job.** The truth is, once you get the dream career or start a new business, you might not feel as happy as you expected, or it might not last as long. This myth is debunked by understanding hedonic adaptation (a.k.a. the hedonic treadmill). The concept of the hedonic treadmill is that we all have a happiness baseline. After we experience a positive event that causes a boost or spike in our happiness, we adapt and return to our standard happiness level. Similarly, if we experience a negative event that lowers our overall happiness level, we'll adapt to that as well and continue on in our new normal. Basically, any achievement that causes a boost in our happiness is only temporary because the mind's tendency is to eventually return to its baseline. The goal here, then, is to raise the baseline so we can experience happiness regardless of what's going on in our lives.

- **I'll be happy when I marry the love of my life.** The truth is, marriage *can* bring happiness into your life, but research suggests that this boost of happiness only lasts an average of two years. Similar to the idea of landing your dream job, you'll get a boost of positive emotions in the beginning, and then guess what? I hope you stretched because you're hopping right back on that hedonic treadmill.

- **I'll be happy once I finally make it (become wealthy)!** The truth is, happiness attracts success, not the other way around like we've been taught to believe. When we feel happy and stress-free, we think clearly, we're more motivated, we communicate better, and we're able to maintain a more positive mindset. These attributes then create space for us to find more success in our relationships and careers.

Now if any of those misconceptions hit home for you, write "ouch" in the margin beside the one that resonated the loudest. Debunking happiness myths isn't something that's new for me, so I understand the punch to the gut that can come from being called out like this.

After starting my love affair with positive psychology in 2015, I began delivering keynote speeches and workshops on the science of happiness at churches, leadership conferences, colleges, and women's events. When kicking off my sessions with these misconceptions, I would get all kinds of reactions. One reaction would be a noticeable lean in with intrigue and curiosity. These folks were easy to keep engaged. I appreciated the affirming head nods and the occasional mouthing of "That makes sense" as they captured their notes. Another reaction I would receive is the folded arms with either clear annoyance or pure skepticism. Listen, this reaction was my favorite! The way my imagination is set up, I felt like I was being challenged to a mental dance-off, and I always keep a heel toe or body roll in my back pocket.

"I know some of y'all saw the title of this session and immediately rolled your eyes," I would start, "but can I tell you a secret? I'm not really here to teach you how to be happy." A few folks would sit a little taller in their seats, and I knew I had piqued their interest. My intention at speaking engagements is to make sure everyone is operating under the same understanding, even for my kindred spirits in the room, and to do so, I tell them exactly what I told you earlier. "I have some good and bad news. The bad news: Negative emotions are inevitable because life isn't picture perfect. Stress happens. Adversity happens. The good news is that positive emotions create a resilient cushion that helps you better deal with stress and adversity." The sugar of the majority of my workshops is happiness and joy, but the medicine is the necessary tool to strengthen folks' resiliency muscles.

If you were to take a stroll through these positive psychology streets, you would find that there isn't one agreed-upon happiness definition or framework that all academics buy into across the board. However, in her book, *The How of Happiness*, popular happiness researcher Sonja Lyubomirsky wrote, "[Happiness is] the experience of joy, contentment, or positive well-being, combined with a sense that one's life is good, meaningful, and worthwhile."[2] I love the phrase "good, meaningful, and worthwhile" because it doesn't make it sound like life has to be perfect. Rather, what's more important is that it is impactful. Of course, there isn't one singular pathway to happiness, but I believe the ultimate goal of this work is to grant yourself permission to be a perfectly imperfect human. I want to park it right here for a moment, because the word *happiness* is tossed around so much and I want you to feel like you have a solid foundation of what it actually means versus what society has told you what it should look like.

Within positive psychology, there are many schools that point to happiness falling within one of two categories: individualistic (focusing more on personal satisfaction and pleasure) or altruistic (focusing more on meaning and life purpose). My belief on happiness is that you can have a healthy balance between the two schools of thought to ensure your life is both meaningful and worthwhile. My personal approach is heavily influenced by Dr. Martin Seligman's theory on Authentic Happiness. We can experience three kinds of happiness: pleasure and gratification, strength and virtue, and finally, meaning and purpose.[3] I like to look at these as dimensions of happiness the way a juggler would approach his juggling act. The first ball is where I'm able to cultivate happiness through focusing on activities that help me to have a more pleasant life experience. In real life, this could look like taking myself out for a slice of pizza in Old Town Alexandria, taking a seat by the water, and mindfully eating the pizza one bite at a time. Once I achieve this first ball, I would then add the second ball where I can focus on activities that help me to develop my strengths and tap into my values. One of my strengths is curiosity, which encourages me to be a student of wisdom and knowledge. I experience enjoyment and satisfaction from reading a new book or exploring a new podcast. If you're interested in seeing a full list of strengths to reference on your own time, you can go to my website at chiantilomax.com/evolve to get a resource that shares them all, including their associated values.

The final ball I add is meaning and purpose. Although it's totally fine to focus on happiness from those other two perspectives, you don't want to get stuck in the pursuit of pleasure, so my advice is to add this last ball to this juggling act. You want to use your unique strengths to be of service to something bigger than yourself. Make it a point to be of service within your community, your faith-based community, or a local school—anywhere of interest that also benefits improving the life of others. This holistic perspective allows happiness to feel more tangible and less fleeting.

When you think back to the myths and misconceptions we discussed earlier, you'll find that most of them are rooted in the idea that you will feel satisfied once your outer circumstances change. Welp! That's fake news. In 2005, Sonja Lyubomirsky, Kennon Sheldon, and David Schkade authored a popular research study of over two thousand twins separated at birth from the Minnesota Twin Registry.[4] This study revealed that our happiness set point (or baseline) is mostly attributed to our genetic disposition (about 50 percent), with intentional activity (what we do, think, and feel) and external circumstance (career, relationships, etc.) following—40 percent and 10 percent, respectively. These three subgroups make up what they call the Life Satisfaction Pie (or the Happiness Pie), and I'm not going to lie to you, it's one of my favorite topics to teach in my workshops. You know Black folks love to blame things on one side of the family: "You must have gotten that from your momma side."

Inheriting traits and characteristics that influence our happiness set point allows that popular familial phrase to take on a whole new meaning, and I was shocked to learn that it had such a strong correlation with our overall life satisfaction.

When this pie was first introduced to me, it made me feel like I had more ownership over my happiness. This idea—that 40 percent of what I do on a daily, weekly, or even monthly basis can increase my life satisfaction—was revolutionary for me at the time. It made me feel more powerful in the face of generational traumas that I didn't have a say in because of what my grandparents or parents had been through. It's not the complete answer to inherited Black trauma, but it's a great start. If you're looking for where to begin, you can even apply the three dimensions of happiness as you consider what intentional actions you want to focus on for cultivating happiness. Ask yourself: What types of intentional actions might bring me pleasure? What kinds of activities can I participate in where I can develop my strengths? Or you can ask yourself, what can I do to be of service to my local community or people around me? As long as you land somewhere between those three questions, you will experience the positive emotions that will help to boost your life satisfaction within that 40 percent.

And hey, don't get caught up in trying to think about the *perfect list of things to do*. Intentional activity doesn't have to be this grandiose action you take on a daily basis. Intentional activity might look like sitting down on Sunday evenings and journaling your top three intentions for the week. Intentional activity might look like waking up every morning and sitting on your front porch. Intentional activity might look like lighting a candle at the end of each workday as you sit and drink a cup of chamomile tea. Intentional activity might look like doing your weekly best friend check-in. If you're trying to find additional support for your 40 percent, I want to share with you one easy personal litmus test. This test is for the folks who want to make sure their intentional activities aren't just things they read on social media, but actual activities that are authentic to what brings them happiness. You want to first consider what it feels like to do the activity every week for an extended period of time. You then want to define your reason for wanting to do it. Questions to reflect on would be: *If I do this for more than a week, will it make me feel lighter or at peace, or will it feel like just another thing on my checklist? How much would I value this activity? How much would I enjoy it? How natural would it feel for me to do it? How much of my reason to keep doing this is because I would feel guilty if I didn't or because someone else wants me to do it?* When you are able to answer those questions for yourself, you can focus on the activities that you truly value, enjoy, and feel natural. You can practice this litmus test a little later in the chapter when you get a chance to create your own custom list.

Years after the release of that study, the researchers have fought in the comments about the breakdown of the percentages. For example, the 2019 research paper, "Easy as (Happiness) Pie," by Nicholas Brown and Julia Rohrer, says that 70 to 80 percent of your happiness levels can be attributed to genetic factors. But even after catching flak from other researchers about the percentages, Lyubomirsky and her crew still maintain that the Happiness Pie is valid and the fact still remains that we have the power to influence and shift our happiness levels rather than rely so heavily on external circumstances. I'm inclined to agree with her!

Before I transferred my membership to the Positive Psychology AME Church of Zion, I was a dedicated member of the "I'll be happy when . . ." ministry. I wasted a lot of time waiting on happiness to show itself. I just knew that all I had to do was move to the big city, meet a Nasir Jones look-alike, buy a home, have a few little ones running around, and boom, life would be complete. I believed there was a finish line I needed to reach in order to experience true joy. With the knowledge I've gained over the years, my view on happiness has drastically changed, and it honestly has little to do with what's going on outside of me. In this season of my life, happiness feels like having a peaceful day even when I wake up on the wrong side of the bed. It feels like being present and engaged on a daily basis, and it feels like making time to do one or two activities a day that energize me and bring me joy. It's the intentionality for me.

As a positive psychology practitioner, my mission is to help you uncover what works best for you. A best practice is to consistently maintain an inventory of activities, experiences, and people that support your overall well-being. This list is subject to change every now and then, so be sure to revisit it as needed.

Before we close out this chapter, I challenge you to create a list of your go-to happiness activities (intentional activity). Do you remember our shady friend, the hedonic treadmill? Well, having a variety of activities in your happiness arsenal is the cheat code to overcoming it. Remember, we're wired to adapt to things that give us a boost of happiness, so if you switch the game up often, you can keep the good vibes flowing longer. Let's be clear: I'm not preaching any toxic "happiology." My hope for you is that you enter this phase of self-discovery with a beginner's mindset and become an active participant in creating more satisfaction in your life. Stay curious about what you're learning and how these tools can bring more balance to your areas of well-being. You never want to force change, so give yourself some grace and approach this practice with an open heart and mind. If you do this, you will experience an organic shift on both the inside and outside.

It's not realistic to believe you will be happy all the time, but with the right tools and intentions, you can create more moments of joy and meaning and lead a more resilient life. Don't close the book just yet! Try this chapter challenge, then feel free to take a much-needed break.

CHAPTER CHALLENGE

There are two parts to this chapter challenge. First, you will get clear on what's adding to your life satisfaction, then you will make a list of activities you can tap into when your hedonic treadmill starts to Milly Rock its way into your daily routine. Listen, this challenge might take a little time, so I recommend you find a quiet place in your home and grab your beverage of choice and something to record your responses with. Set aside at least fifteen minutes to complete these reflections.

Remember that intentional activity plays a very influential role in your Happiness Pie, your overall life satisfaction. So let's take the next step and take inventory of your happiness picture. Before you begin the following exercises, ask yourself, *What activities do I currently do on a regular basis that bring me joy?* These activities might include having a cup of coffee in the morning before everyone in your home wakes up, running errands for your retired neighbor once a week, or maybe you enjoy a hip-hop dance class on Friday nights. Consider anything that lifts your mood when you're having a not-so-great-week. Next, consider what unfavorable activities or habits you need to leave out of your Happiness Pie to lessen feelings of dissatisfaction. This could be anything from talking on the phone to a toxic family member, doom scrolling, or even hanging out with a group of friends when you would rather sit on the couch and watch *Martin* reruns. If you need to, refer back to your well-being scores from the chapter check-in on page 17 and notice what influenced your scores. This can help you complete part one of this activity.

Part 1: Happy Hour
Happiness Inventory Check

The Invitation: Review the following questions and honestly record your responses. Be sure to list experiences, moments, or interactions that take away from your happiness.

What's Blocking My Happy?
In a journal or tablet, create three columns on a blank page.

- In the first column, write down what makes you unhappy. Aim for at least ten items in this list.

- In the second column, rank your unhappy activities/ moments from 1 to 5, with 1 being "It's mildly annoying" and 5 being "I feel awful during this."

- For each item, ask yourself: "Do I have the ability to change this?"

- For the items you can change, write down how you do so in the third column. Start with one or two ways to shift this in the right direction.

> **UNHAPPY INVENTORY GROW TIP:** If you need help identifying what's decreasing your happiness levels, consider asking yourself:
>
> - What's currently draining my energy?
>
> - What is preventing me from feeling joy and excitement?
>
> - What is causing me the most stress and anxiety right now?

What's Making Me Happy?

In a journal or tablet, create three columns on a blank page.

- In the first column, write down what brings you happiness. Aim for at least ten items in this list.

- In the second column, rank your happy activities/moments from 1 to 5, with 1 being a happiness snack and 5 being a full-course happiness meal.

- For each item, ask yourself if you have the ability to change how often you engage in this activity.

- In the third column, write down how you plan to complete the high-scoring activities more often in your life.

Pause for Reflection: Before you move to the next part of this challenge, pause for a moment and reflect on what came up for you as you examined your happiness inventory. What did you notice? How did you feel? What challenges, if any, came up for you? What surprised you as you were completing each inventory? Set a timer for five to seven minutes and capture these reflections in your journal. When you've gotten all your thoughts out, feel free to move on to the next part.

Part 2: Happy Catalog
Your Top 10 Happiness List

The Invitation: Now it's time to map out your intentional activity. Based on the output of your happiness inventory check, create a list of ten of your go-to joy-inducing, laughter-bringing, smile-fostering, and energy-slinging activities that you can commit to incorporating into your daily life. Feel free to get creative here and perhaps even switch out some activities that feel outdated.

To help you get started, here is a cheat sheet of research-based intentional activities, brought to you by Sonja Lyubomirsky, that are known to increase life satisfaction. When taking a peek at her list, only consider activities that feel natural, bring genuine enjoyment, or add value to your overall happiness. Don't feel obligated to choose anything because it's what you think you *should* do. Your goal is to create a list of happiness-boosting activities that will honor *your* version of happiness.

- Express gratitude
- Cultivate optimism
- Avoid overthinking and social comparison
- Practice acts of kindness
- Nurture relationships
- Develop healthy coping strategies (e.g., spend time with your friends, go for a walk, journal about your feelings)
- Lean into forgiveness of yourself and other people
- Replay and savor life's joys
- Set and commit to your goals
- Practice your spirituality
- Take care of your body

Remember, authentic happiness is a continuous journey that thrives on intentional actions and self-awareness. It's not about creating a picture-perfect life, but it does require you to create space for moments of reflection and a wholehearted commitment to nurturing your well-being. In the next chapter, we'll spend time exploring the transformative power of a growth mindset, which will help you approach your happiness with a more grounded viewpoint. Are you ready to continue this journey toward self-mastery together? Let's get going!

CHAPTER 3

FREE YOUR MIND
AND THE REST WILL FOLLOW

Using Your Mindset as a Superpower

The next student coming to the stage is Chiaaaaaantiiiiii Lomaaaaaaaax!"
This was my moment. I was so excited, but also very focused as I walked
onto the stage of my very first Mauldin Elementary talent show. I still
remember the outfit I wore: a white blouse with a red skirt covered with silver flowers (special shout-out to Momma Lomax for coming through with
the Sears special). The hit song "Candy Rain" by Soul for Real had taken the
radio by storm in 1994, and your girl was totally caught up in their rapture. I
knew every single lyric, ad lib, and the whole dance routine from the music
video. Yes, including that little one-two shoulder bop and stutter step! To
this day, it's one of my go-to songs on my happiness playlist when I need a
good mental and emotional pick-me-up, and you're absolutely going to get
these off-key notes at the top of my lungs every single time.

I remember that day like it was yesterday. In fifth grade, I had the
audacity to sign up for the talent show and sing this four-part harmony song *alone* in front of the entire school, which included teachers,

classmates, and their parents. My mom couldn't make it because she had to work, but I was a resourceful and spunky kid. I think many of us were in my neighborhood. As latchkey kids, many of us tapped into strategy and creativity super early. It was the life we knew.

Let me set the scene for you. It was an early evening talent show, and I was silently rehearsing the lyrics in my head as I sat next to my friend and her mom who had given me a ride to the school. After a few kids had performed, it was my time to shine. I sauntered my way up to the stage, the music started, and my inner Rhythm Nation jumped out. I had stage presence and crowd participation. People in the audience were snapping their fingers, clapping their hands, and bobbing their heads to the beat. I knew I killed it.

But that was me. I was the kid at the functions who would get up to dance and sing when aunties and grandma would say, "Baby, get up there and show them that move you know how to do." Ten-year-old Chianti was a superstar. One of my summer camp counselors at the Phyllis Wheatley Recreation Center even nicknamed me "Electric Boogaloo" because at any moment I would bust out my dance moves like no one was watching (or maybe because I knew everyone was watching). I loved being me and being free.

What I loved most about ten-year-old Chianti was her belief of self. She believed that if she thought about it, she could make it happen, even for something like a school-wide talent show. She made sure to memorize all the lyrics of the song she wanted to sing, and she knew that making time to practice every day after school leading up to the show would give her the confidence she needed to perform. And when it was showtime, she did what needed to be done: rocked the hell out of that stage. Just as a side note: If you're invested in this story, I want to let you know that, unfortunately, I didn't win first place, but I was proud of my performance. I worked hard on it, I believed in myself, and it showed. Without even realizing it, I was cultivating my relationship with my strongest superpower: my mindset.

Another tool I attribute to my early development is music. I tell people all the time that hip-hop was like another character in my childhood story. She wasn't always right or wise, but she meant well. As an adult, I realize I first learned about the practices of visualization and positive thinking through hip-hop. Now before you go all *hip-hop is filled with misogyny*, I'm very aware. I'm also very aware that for many Black children who grew up in low-income neighborhoods, hip-hop was our first, and sometimes only, glimpse into a better way of life, a life filled with financial independence, homeownership, and entrepreneurship. Before I moved away from home, it gave me exposure to images of Black men and women succeeding and thriving. Hip-hop was my first glimpse at what it meant to thrive in a country that wasn't built for people who looked like me.

Now, I know, I know, it didn't always have positive messaging, but with the mom and older brother I had, I was always tapped into a good balance of conscious and boom bap. I knew all the good stuff: Nas, EPMD, Common, Queen Latifah, MC Lyte, Foxy Brown, Mos Def, Talib Kweli, Big L, Big Pun, Tupac, Biggie, The Fugees, and the list goes on. Biggie told me that the sky was the limit, Tupac told me to keep my head up, Talib said I had to keep on dancing, and Mos Def reminded me that even in the face of adversity, I had to shine my light for the world to see. This helped inform my beliefs around persistence and growth early on and is what I consider to be the early stages of my growth mindset. Not only did music play a major role in dropping positive seeds into my thoughts, but my education story continued to influence my "can do" attitude.

Third grade was a pivotal year in my academic career, as it was the first time I was positively acknowledged by my teacher (one of the few black teachers in my school) instead of reprimanded for being a child. You see, I would often finish my classwork before other students and kill time by talking to my friends in my surrounding cluster of desks. As you can imagine, this was annoying for my teacher to deal with, but instead of seeing me as a troublemaker, my teacher believed that my ability to finish work ahead of schedule was a sign that I needed to be challenged. So she sent a letter home to speak with my mom about putting me in more advanced classes in fourth grade. Her belief and my mom's trust in me helped boost my confidence. I remember receiving my first advanced math test from my new math teacher, thinking to myself, *Good lord, what did I get myself into?* But then I had a second thought: *If my mom and teacher think I can do this, the least I can do is just try.* So I did. I may not have been the top student in those advanced classes, but with their encouragement, I believed I could do challenging things.

My "can do" mindset traveled with me in other seasons of my life as you can imagine. Of course I went on to rock the stage at the school-wide talent show like I was on an episode of *Teen Summit,* but it also gave me the courage to try things outside of my comfort zone. My mom belonged to the "keep these kids occupied at all costs" congregation, so it is not a surprise that I was part of several after-school programs and youth organizations. I had my most memorable experience with the Girl Scouts.

My troop leader reached out to my mom one day informing her that I was handpicked to do a local television commercial about conserving electricity. My mom put the phone down, looked at me, and asked, "Is this something you think you can do?" I remember looking up at her saying, "I don't know, but I can try." Weeks later, I was on set with a fresh set of braids and beads and my lines memorized.

In his book, *Learned Optimism,* Martin Seligman defines a positive mindset as "approaching life's challenges with a positive outlook. It doesn't mean ignoring or avoiding difficult situations. Having a positive mindset means making the most of potential obstacles, trying to see the best in people, and viewing yourself and your abilities in a positive light." There were so many experiences and moments in my childhood that could have led me down a less favorable path. If I'd allowed my environment to define me, I would have never jumped on that stage at the talent show. If I'd adopted a negative mindset, I would never have accepted the educational challenges. If I'd had a negative mindset, I would have never been able to do the Girl Scouts commercial and use my voice to talk about important things. Leaning into a positive mindset around my abilities gave me the curiosity and courage to rise to the occasion throughout my childhood and adult years. And for that,

I'm grateful. Before we deconstruct what your personal mindset is, let's unpack where mindsets come from in the first place.

Our mindset is the set of beliefs or ways of thinking that determine our behavior, overall outlook on life, and mental attitude. Your mindset is formed by various factors in your life, the most notable being your upbringing, religious communities, and media. As a result, it influences how we navigate relationships, finances, business, parenting, and even the acquisition of knowledge. Although I was inclined to lean more toward the brighter side of things as a child, I couldn't fully escape the influence of everything around me. I've had moments where my mindset was a hindrance instead of a helper in getting me the best outcomes. I'm sure you could name a few instances for yourself as well.

Here's a piece of truth that might sting: Every thought that comes to your mind is not a fact. Some thoughts we have may be *based* on factual details, but the full scope of the thought could also be a result of outside interferences, like social norms, collective narratives, or identities we adopt from our parents and communities. For example, you may have been told things like, "You should greet everyone," "Say 'yes, sir' and 'yes, ma'am' when responding to people who are your senior," "People who grew up differently from you will never understand where you're coming from," "Never talk to strangers about what happens in your home," and most importantly "Ranch dressing is used on all salads, your pizza, and wings." I became aware of most of these social norms and narratives when I moved further away from home. Now, as a more tenured DMV resident, I know there is a time and a place for greeting people in public places, some of my closest confidants are friends who grew up with different family dynamics than my own, and not keeping ranch in my home is one of the healthiest decisions I've made to date. Learning how to accurately decipher the difference between fact and opinion is the first step in reframing the limiting beliefs that do not honor your personal transformation.

With that being said, let's check in.

CHAPTER CHECK-IN

The way you think is a catalyst for what will either propel you forward or hold you back. As a result, mindset is one of the main pillars in my coaching and training programs. I even named one of group coaching programs Marathon Mindset (shout-out to Nipsey). In true coaching form, I'd like to create space in this moment for you to put a microscope on your own thoughts.

The Invitation: Think about a time when you didn't go after an opportunity. This could have been a personal opportunity, like a new friendship, a romantic partner, or a career/business opportunity.

- During this time, what thoughts were going through your head?

- What convinced you to not take the chance?

- What did you think might happen if you *did* take the chance?

Without overthinking, spend the next three to five minutes writing the first things that come to mind. When the time is up, read over what you wrote down, and beside each item, write either "fact" or "fiction."

Now that we're checked in, let's dig in to how we can reframe these limiting beliefs and improve our overall mindset. Admittedly, I'm *still* unlearning beliefs and behaviors that are accomplices to doubt, self-sabotage, and fear. Some thoughts and beliefs shed quicker than others, and that's OK. Change takes time. So please show yourself some grace during this process. Slow progress is still progress.

People typically believe you either have a positive or negative mindset, but researcher Carol Dweck, another one of my positive psychology besties in my mind, shares that there are two types of mindsets: growth and fixed. The great news is you do not permanently have just one type; at any time, you have the ability to shift from one mindset to the other.

Generally, people with fixed mindsets believe everyone is born with a set of qualities and abilities. They subscribe to the limited belief of "you either have it or you don't." People with a growth mindset, on the other hand, believe there is always something to learn and a way to improve. They are okay with being a student and not having all of the answers from jump.

Fixed Mindset:	Growth Mindset:
Judging Perspective	Learning Perspective
I can't learn anything new.	*I can learn and grow if I invest enough effort.*
Typically achieve less than their full potential.	Typically reach a higher level of achievement.

Let's walk through a few examples for each. A person with a fixed mindset generally has a judgmental perspective that is mainly focused on the outcome of a situation. This typically keeps them from trying new things out of fear of embarrassment, and they may talk badly about themselves when they fail; if they succeed, they may believe they have nothing else to learn. But a person with a growth mindset sees every opportunity and challenge in life as a learning opportunity, focusing on the process as a whole instead of just the outcome. This person will typically see new challenges as a way to grow, will vow to work harder when they fail, and will seek even more ways to expand and learn when they succeed.

Oh, and guess what? It doesn't even stop there. The type of mindset you have can change depending on the area of well-being. For example, you may have a growth mindset regarding your career, but a fixed mindset when it comes to your relationships. This is why you may find you are thriving in one area of well-being and struggling in others. Luckily, mindsets are learned and, therefore, can be changed. You have the ability to improve if it's something you want to do.

CHAPTER CHECK-IN

When I first learned the difference between a growth and fixed mindset, my brain went into overdrive. I remember sitting in my positive psychology class wishing I had a magic pause button so I could spend a few minutes jotting down all the thoughts and connections I was making in the moment. When I teach my workshops around mindset, I get a similar reaction from my attendees—wide eyes, heads tilted to the side, and mouths open followed by a request for extra time to reflect. So it's only right that we pause here to see what's coming up for you.

The Invitation: Set a five-minute timer and reflect on the areas of well-being (financial, social, career, physical, and community/spiritual) in your journal with these prompts:

- In which well-being areas do you hold a fixed mindset? What has influenced this mindset?

- In which well-being areas do you hold a growth mindset? What has influenced this mindset?

When I'm teaching my coaching clients about their fixed mindset, I tell them to treat it like it's their inner hater, and I usually have them give it a name. This personification of the mindset usually makes the work a bit easier to manage. Take a moment to think of a name for your inner hater right now. If you need ideas, you can go with something like Barbara, Shirley, Sam, or Alice.

Once you've identified your mindsets and have given the fixed mindsets a name, there are four simple steps that can help you redirect those mindsets toward a more beneficial way of thinking. I've followed these steps to work through my own limiting beliefs, and it's something I teach in my small group coaching sessions.

> **Step 1: Learn to hear your fixed mindset's voice.** You will notice that once you experience a setback or challenge, your inner hater will say things like, "People who look like us

can't do this," or, "Maybe you're just not cut out for this," or, "What if you fail?"

Step 2: Acknowledge you have a choice. The way you receive setbacks and challenges is your decision. You get to decide if you would like to respond from a place of lack (fixed mindset) or a place of expansion, strategy, and effort (growth mindset). If you get to this step and you find yourself feeling stuck or making excuses for something not working out, the goal is to keep failure in perspective and not fall into a fixed mindset trap. Remind yourself that failure is a normal part of growth. Everyone on the face of this earth has experienced it. Try refocusing on your effort, resources, and ways to improve. Ask yourself questions like: "What is my role in making this successful?" "What is a better way to get this done?" "Who can I ask for honest feedback to get me out of this loop?"

Step 3: Talk back to your inner hater with a growth mindset. Once you've realized what your fixed mindset's voice sounds like, confront it with a growth mindset response. For example, you could say, "Honey, it's OK. Failure is data. If I fail, I will be more prepared for my success the next time around."

Step 4: Take the growth mindset action. As you practice, you'll get better at choosing which voice works best for you. Action looks like seeking constructive feedback, capturing the lessons you learned from failure, or approaching a challenge head on. Just remember that you always have a choice.

GROW TIP: Take a few minutes to revisit the fixed mindsets you captured in your check-in and run them through those four steps to practice holding your inner hater accountable.

Would you believe me if I told you it gets even deeper than this? In addition to holding you back mentally, your mindset can become a self-fulfilling prophecy for better or worse. The Berkeley Well-Being Institute defines a self-fulfilling prophecy as a belief that leads you to act a certain way, causing the expected outcome of what you believed. Essentially, when your beliefs are left unchecked, it creates a cycle that influences the outcome. When you think something bad or good will happen, your thoughts will influence how you act, which will usually manifest your thoughts into reality. You can have a negative self-fulfilling prophecy or a positive one; it all depends on the direction of your beliefs and expectations.

When I explain this to my coaching clients, I like to visually draw out this cycle of gloom or doom depending on how their beliefs unfold. I like to start with their belief about a scenario. This belief can be positive or negative. The beliefs we possess will influence how we show up, what we do, and what we say. The next part of the cycle is determined by how others receive our actions. Our actions essentially determine what others think of us in the scenario that causes (or influences) their behavior towards us. Your original belief about yourself or the situation may be positively or negatively reinforced by how the people in your scenario respond to you. This is the self-fulfilling prophecy cycle. If you believe you can learn how to do something better, then you will take actions that help you to improve, like reading up on the subject, finding a tutor, or watching informative videos. On the flip side, if you believe you will fail, then you will do things that lead to failure like slacking off or not preparing yourself. Developing a growth mindset will support you in creating self-fulfilling prophecies that contribute to more meaningful and positive life experiences.

THE CYCLE

Our Actions
(toward others)

Influence

Impact

Our Beliefs
(about ourselves)

**SELF-FULFILLING
PROPHECY**

Others' Beliefs
(about us)

Reinforce

Cause

Others' Actions
(towards us)

Let's walk through an example of a negative self-fulfilling prophecy cycle.

- **Initial belief:** Issa believes she is never going to get a promotion at work.

- **Actions:** Because of her belief, she no longer looks for opportunities to grow her skillset, she barely engages with her coworkers outside of meetings, and she never volunteers for additional responsibilities.

- **Others' beliefs:** Her supervisor Molly starts to believe that Issa is content with her current role as an individual contributor.

- **Others' actions (a.k.a. The Moment of Truth):** When annual reviews roll around, Molly does not add Issa's name to the list of team members to consider for the new team lead promotion.

- **The belief afterward:** Because of her lack of effort and drive, Issa remains in her role for another year. She feels like she will never get the chance to move up the ladder at her current place of work.

Let's walk through an example of my own positive self-fulfilling prophecy cycle.

- **My initial belief/mindset:** I want to host a happiness experience for millennials that feels like a playdate for adults. I don't have any help, and I'm not sure who will show up, but I think it would be a really dope experience.

- **My actions:** I enlisted a friend who specializes in event planning and sponsorships and asked other friends if they would like to be volunteers to help on the day of the event.

- **Others' beliefs/mindset:** We had over one hundred RSVPs within seven days of announcing the pop-up. I received tons of text messages and emails from folks sharing their anticipation for the event.

- **Other's actions (a.k.a. The Moment of Truth):** Seventy-five Black and brown millennials attended and stayed for the entire three-hour event. The responses we received from the post-event survey were overwhelmingly positive.

- **My belief afterward:** With the right support, I can host entertaining, engaging, and educational events that people will love.

CHAPTER CHECK-IN

The Invitation: Before we close out this chapter, I want to pause for a few minutes to explore what this idea of a self-fulfilling prophecy means in your personal life.

- Revisit your responses from the fixed mindset check-in and note which area you are struggling with the most.

- What self-fulfilling prophecies, if any, have you experienced in this area?

- What beliefs or set of beliefs would you like to adopt to ensure you have a more favorable outcome in the future?

GRACE REMINDER: After the work you've done in this chapter, I would say you have earned a break. Treat yourself to a full-body stretch, a cup of tea, or a few deep, cleansing breaths. It's totally up to you.

Your mindset is one of the most important things to cultivate throughout this self-discovery journey. Without it, it can be very easy to fall into destructive cycles that keep you in a loop of negativity and lack. Now that you have this foundational knowledge on how you can switch your fixed mindset to a growth-oriented one, let's move on to the next chapter, where we'll cover how to use optimism and mindfulness as weapons of mass construction against your mind chatter.

CHAPTER 4

MIND OVER MIND CHATTER

Fighting Negativity with Optimism and Mindfulness

I have a very familiar relationship with negative mind chatter. I try not to mingle with her too much, but every now and then, she catches me slipping on a humble day.

A few years back, I was at the end of my apartment lease and needed to make a decision on my next housing situation. In my mind, I only had two options: I could stay in the current apartment building with Mickey Mouse, who was hanging out in a wall near my kitchen (I'd heard from other neighbors that they were having the same issues), or I could find another super expensive apartment in Alexandria, where rental prices were skyrocketing each year. Since I didn't feel like sharing a kitchen with Mickey and Minnie, I decided to find a realtor to help me get a deal on a condo to rent anywhere else in the DMV area. With the help of social media and a few internet reviews, I landed on a highly recommended realtor who seemed to really know her stuff. I immediately shared that I was hoping to rent a property anywhere in the metro area that was within a certain price range. After gathering key financial details, she posed a question that caught me off guard.

"Have you ever considered buying property instead of renting it?" she asked.

"Uh, maybe one day in the future, but no, I hadn't thought about it for this current move," I said.

She assured me that with my current financial picture, I could get a really affordable condo and a monthly mortgage that was not only within my price range, but much lower than what I was willing to pay for rent.

If I'm being completely transparent, in my picture-perfect world, I was hoping to be married before I purchased my first home. Chile, I know. I'm judging myself as I share this memory with you. Not only did the realtor's proposal not fit my picture-perfect life, but in my mind, buying a home wasn't something I could do as an individual. For some reason, I had already made up my mind that my credit score wasn't good enough and I didn't make enough money. Girl, it's the full telenovela storyline for me. I shared with her both of those thoughts, and she lovingly pushed back, sharing the benefits of homeownership and how I should speak with a home loan officer to look into my options.

Soon enough, I received a call from the loan officer at a credit union who revealed that my credit score was in the high 700s and that my salary made me an ideal candidate for a home loan. The only thing I could say to him was, "Say what now?" I was both surprised and proud of myself! Your girl was about to embark on the homebuying journey. The only person in my immediate family that owned their home was my paternal grandfather, so this was BIG to me. By early November, I was moving into my new place, a home I could call my own.

This experience brought a profound realization: my thoughts and self-imposed limitations had prevented me from pursuing homeownership sooner. I had allowed negative beliefs and self-doubt to deter me from even considering the possibility. However, once I managed to break free from the confines of my mind, I recognized that I could have embarked on this journey long ago. It served as a compelling reminder that often the biggest obstacle we face is not external circumstances but our own inner hater, our fixed mindset voice that whispers, "You can't do it."

As I began this new chapter of my life as a homeowner, I committed myself to consistently confronting and challenging my negative thinking patterns. I'm sure you can relate to the impact of negative mind chatter and how it can prevent you from pursuing your dreams and reaching your full potential. We are going to spend this chapter learning how to overcome these irrational thinking patterns and self-limiting beliefs because, sis, we have glamorous goals to reach and beautiful lives to create. I want to make sure you aren't the reason you don't get there.

In the previous chapter, we got a brief introduction to your mind chatter (fixed mindset), named this inner hater, and learned how adopting a growth mindset could help you create more favorable self-fulfilling prophecies. You may be feeling overwhelmed by all the new information, but remember that the mind chatter that exists within us today didn't develop overnight, so don't expect to fix everything all at once.

One of the secrets to being more present and thoughtful in your journey is to become besties with your mind chatter. This will help you become better at separating the truth from any outdated belief systems you might be harboring. Acquainting yourself with your inner hater on this level will require you to dig deeper into the origin of your thoughts. This chapter will give you the tools to befriend your mind chatter and reframe and redirect those harmful thoughts before they manifest themselves in the world as self-fulfilling prophecies.

In positive psychology, learned helplessness is a concept that describes when you feel powerless over a situation after you've consistently experienced negative life events. Over time, you might even adopt the belief that you don't have much control over anything that happens to you, contributing to an overall feeling of helplessness or even depression. For example, our good friend Issa believed that career advancement wasn't in the cards for her. Since she was looked over year after year for promotion, she felt like putting forth any type of effort at work would be pointless. So she stopped engaging with her team members, volunteering for additional responsibilities, and just gave up on the idea that she would ever be promoted.

Clinical psychologist Lyn Abramson and a few of her really smart researcher friends introduced an updated version of learned helplessness that digs into how people cope and explain things that are out of their control.[1] Basically, when you come up against situations that aren't in your control, your brain attempts to make sense of the situation by developing a consistent way to explain what's happening to you, which can either be optimistic or pessimistic (positive or negative). This way of making sense of your circumstances is known as your *explanatory style*.[2] Your explanatory style influences your mindset, how you respond to situations, and can impact how you show up in personal and professional relationships.

Let's say you have a close friend named Zaya who is fed up with her job. You've been helping her prepare for interviews, so you're tapped into her process extensively. She has been on seven job interviews, and six months later, there is still no job offer in sight. One day while you're helping her prepare for her next interview, she rips up her résumé and says, "I suck at interviews. I'm never going to find a new job." You leave her alone to stew in her thoughts, and over coffee a few weeks later, you ask her for an update on her job search. She says that she stopped going to interviews because no one was going to hire her anyway. The baffling part to you is that you've seen Zaya take a similar stance with dating. "I'm not looking for a relationship because they are doomed to fail anyway." Not only has Zaya adopted a fixed mindset around job hunting and dating, but because of being let down so many times, Zaya has turned into a pessimist, automatically expecting the worst because of what has happened to her in the past. This is her mind's way of protecting her from future hurt, but in reality, it's keeping her stagnant and unhappy.

When pessimism joins forces with our mind chatter in this way, it's time to plan a counterattack. I know that sounds so extra, but you know me, I'm all about the theatrics in the spirit of helping a sister out. If you find yourself feeling a tad bit like Zaya these days, you should try on the concept of *learned optimism*. Learned optimism, a term coined by Martin Seligman (remember, he is a pioneer of positive psychology), is the opposite of *learned helplessness*. Seligman believed that optimism can be taught as a strategy to help us become more resilient in the face of adversity. One of my favorite quotes from him is, "Life inflicts the same setbacks and tragedies on the optimist as on the pessimist, but the optimist weathers them better."[3] Learned optimism is a principle that teaches us to identify negative mind chatter and destructive thinking patterns and transform them into more positive and constructive thoughts. So in Zaya's case, with a touch of learned optimism, she could learn how to challenge her inner hater and approach her job search and dating life with a lot more hope and resilience, even if the situation seems bleak at face value.

Here's the thing. There are so many ways to become a more optimistic person, but the strategy I teach in my workshops and to my clients is the ABC model within learned optimism. Before we dig into this model, I want to first break down the three types of inner haters in our minds that trick us into having these negative or flawed perspectives on life and influence our explanatory styles. Let's call them the three decepticons of a balanced reality: personalization, pervasiveness, and permanence. When they are left unchecked, these decepticons run rampant, causing all kinds of issues in our day-to-day lives.

Personalization is when you blame yourself for a negative event or failure. You don't really consider the external factors that played a part in the setback. If we pan the camera back to Zaya, we'll recognize that she really believes she is terrible at interviews and hasn't considered that external issues could be preventing her from securing a position, such as culture fit or skill set. If she were tapped into her optimist bag, she would chalk this failure up as a temporary setback and look forward to getting back at it the next time around.

Pervasiveness is when you think a negative experience or failure applies across all areas of life. This mind trick will have you believing your whole life is trash just because you had one bad day. I know you've been there. Maybe you ate something you weren't supposed to on a diet, or you missed your train to work. All of a sudden, it's five o'clock and you're still reeling from something that happened at 8 am.

Permanence is when you think the bad experience or failure will last always and forever. In the case of Zaya, she believed that because she hadn't found a job yet, she would never find one. Do you see how this kind of thinking will keep someone trapped in a negative self-fulfilling prophecy?

Now that we know what the types of inner haters are that influence our explanatory styles, let's break down how the ABC model can help us identify our unrealistic beliefs, challenge them, and reframe them to be more balanced and optimistic. The goal is to help you better manage your emotions and actions, which will naturally create better circumstances.

The ABC model teaches us that emotions are not caused by an external event; instead, our beliefs about this external event are what influences how we feel or act. The three main parts of this model are the **Activating** event (this can be a negative or positive circumstance), our **Beliefs** about said event (rational or irrational interpretations), and the **Consequences** of those beliefs (your feelings and responses).[4] This model shows us that if your mind chatter is full of irrational beliefs, you will experience negative emotions in response to a challenging situation. However, by using ABC as a technique to talk back to your mind chatter, you can shift your behaviors and perspective to one that's more beneficial for well-being and growth.

Okay, so let's circle back to our good sis Zaya and walk her example through the ABC model so she can challenge her inner haters.

Scenario: Zaya has been on seven job interviews, and six months later, there is still no job offer in sight. A feedback email finally arrived from the company where she had her last interview a month ago.

A. **Activating Event:** Zaya does not get the job.

B. **Beliefs:** Zaya believes, "I suck at interviews. I'm never going to find a new job."

C. **Consequences:** Zaya feels discouraged, sad, and terrible about herself and doesn't plan on applying for another job for the rest of the year.

From Zaya's current perspective, you can see that she has personalized this event (*I suck at interviews*) and is leaning into a bit of permanence as well (*I'm never going to find a new job*).

Once you've identified the activating event, your beliefs surrounding the event, and the consequences of those beliefs, the next part of the

ABC process is to **Dispute** the negative mind chatter (especially the irrational thoughts or beliefs) and replace it with more productive thoughts. It is like taking your beliefs to court, and it requires you to ask yourself questions to unpack the evidence for or against your negative beliefs. Even if you can only find one piece of evidence against the negative thought, then you know it is false. There's a lot of potential nuances to uncover here, so for the sake of clarity, the disputation process can be broken down into three steps:

1. Identify and define your irrational belief (part B of the model)

2. Search for evidence for or against the belief

3. Develop a more truthful statement to replace the belief

After you dispute your irrational thoughts, then the last part of the process is the result of the dispute, which is known as the new **Effect** (a.k.a. a new belief). When we refuse to accept our irrational thoughts as facts, we can treat them as basic thoughts, reframe them, and take the steps to be more resilient next time around. Although, technically we could refer to the ABC model as the ABCDE model, the last two steps are like the "g" in lasagna. We never say it, but we know it's there.

Now that we have the final two steps of the model, let's walk Zaya through the end of the process so she can move from feeling like a victim with no control over her outcome to an empowered woman who can find her way to her next best step!

A. **Activating Event:** Zaya does not get the job.

B. **Beliefs:** Zaya thinks, "I suck at interviews. I'm never going to find a new job."

C. **Consequence:** Zaya feels discouraged, sad, and terrible about herself and doesn't apply for another job for the rest of the year.

D. **Dispute:** What proves that Zaya's belief is not true? She has worked at three different jobs over the past ten years, which means she has been successful at interviewing before. She has a nursing degree, which is especially good to have in this post-pandemic world; the medical field is always in need of nurses. She has helped two of her friends find jobs by supporting their interview preparation.

New Effective Belief: After challenging her beliefs about her job search, she realizes she's been successful at securing jobs in her field before, so perhaps it's time to follow up with the interviewers to request feedback that can help her prepare for the next interview.

Before I turn you loose with another chapter check-in, let me just say that optimism is not the same as toxic positivity. Optimism does not ignore the fact that adversity and disappointment exist. Remember, with learned optimism, the goal is to help you be more resilient and solution-oriented when faced with challenges.

CHAPTER CHECK-IN

You know the drill by now. Let's pause so you have time to practice this on your own.

The Invitation: Take a moment to reflect on a recent event in your life using the ABC(DE) model. If it helps, focus on one of the well-being categories—career, social, financial, community/spiritual, and physical—to help jog your memory. Set your timer for five to seven minutes and follow the process.

Befriending the ABC Model

A. **Activating Event:** Choose a recent event and list out the details (what, where, and when)

B. **Beliefs:** What thoughts or beliefs came up for you during and after the event?

C. **Consequences:** How did the beliefs make you feel? What did you do or not do because of them?

D. **Dispute:** What proof do you have that your belief surrounding this event is false?

E. **New Effective Belief:** What positive statement can you use to replace that belief? What is your next best step?

The ABC model is a mindset game changer. By using this to break down negative events in your life, not only are you continuing to advance and build your self-awareness skills, but you are also better equipping yourself to release your limiting beliefs and position yourself in the driver's seat of your life experiences.

The ABC model is great on its own, but when you add the practice of mindfulness (which we'll discuss in just a bit), these two tools become like Barack and Michelle Obama. Of course, we loved Barack as president, but the added power of Auntie Michelle brought the administration to the next level of love, flavor, empathy, and passion. Name a better duo—I'll wait. On its own, the ABC model provides us with tools to identify and challenge our negative thinking patterns, but mindfulness gives us the extra support we need to proactively observe and face these thoughts. If you think your arsenal is already packed with tons of transformation goodies, a consistent mindfulness practice is going to turn you into a mental and emotional superhero.

THE POWER OF MINDFULNESS

"Be" by Common is one of my favorite hip-hop album intro songs of all time. There is a lyric at the end of it that has sat in the seat of my soul since it was released. It reminds me to look at the present as a gift and focus on being in the moment. I mean, it also doesn't hurt that he is easy on the eyes, but we can talk about that later over a few glasses of rosé! I might be one of the few people in this world that aligns hip-hop music to self-help practices, but to me these lines, "Never looking back, or too far in front of me. The present is a gift and I just wanna be," embody how I view my personal mindfulness practice.

Mindfulness is a valuable asset to the ABC model, as practicing it on a day-to-day basis will further amplify the condition of your thoughts and behaviors, helping you create a more transformative impact on the way you show up in any facet of life.

You may have heard about mindfulness on social media or in the latest wellness magazines, but oftentimes it's not clearly defined for us, so I want to start with a basic understanding of what mindfulness is and what mindfulness is not.

Mindfulness is the practice of intentionally directing your attention to the present moment and approaching every situation with gentleness and without judgment, allowing things to unfold without trying to change anything. To "be in the moment" is to be fully present and engaged in what is happening within yourself and the environment around you. In that moment, you are paying attention to your thoughts and emotions, how you feel in your body, and whatever else is happening outside of your body. This is important because so many of us are currently living life on autopilot, and if we don't take the time to appreciate the little moments, we may wake one day to find that life has completely passed us by.

For instance, have you ever been on your way home from work, only to find that you don't even remember the actual drive once you get to your destination? You know you've passed traffic lights and construction zones and you may have even dodged a few potholes, but somehow you were completely blanked out. This has definitely happened to me, and it made me feel a little uneasy when I realized how much my mind can zone out during such an important task. My driving experience when I'm mindful versus when I'm on autopilot is completely different. It's much more entertaining when I'm tapped into the drive. When I'm driving mindfully, I notice everything, including my bodily sensations and how tight my hips might feel from sitting all day at work. I notice new construction sites in my area. I notice other drivers singing in their cars. I notice drivers beside me at the light that might appear stressed or happy. I even notice restaurants I've never tried before. I'm always having those "Dang, I didn't know we had a *insert random restaurant* around here" moments.

So being "in the moment" is not about putting up blinders to everyday life; in fact, it's the opposite. It's tuning into everyday life and making sure you're engaged in it moment by moment. When I'm more mindful, my emails to clients are more clear, my conversations with friends are more thoughtful, my workouts are more fulfilling, and my walks are more adventurous. If you approach each well-being area more mindfully, you will find yourself being more productive, more detail-oriented, and more in tune with things you'd otherwise miss when you're operating on autopilot.

When I practice mindfulness myself or when I lead a mindfulness practice for a group of people, I like to follow a few basic guidelines to help set the tone for the moment: free yourself from any expectations; refrain from judging yourself and other people; lean into being an observer of your thoughts, emotions, and bodily sensations; and most importantly, approach each mindfulness practice with a beginner's mindset. When you do this, all the other guidelines will fall into place because you won't be expecting the same experience.

Mindfulness Misconceptions

Because mindfulness is so popular, there are a few common misconceptions floating about in the self-care universe that I'd love to take a moment to clear up.

- **Mindfulness is a religious practice:** Yes, mindfulness has roots in Eastern religious practices; however, the practice itself is secular and unattached to any particular religion. You can practice mindfulness regardless of who or what you believe in.

- **Mindfulness is the same as meditation:** Although they are often used interchangeably, mindfulness and meditation are not the same thing. Meditation is a structured practice that focuses on a specific object, idea, or quieting the mind in general. Mindfulness, on the other hand, is a practice rooted in staying in the present moment. In this way, you can be mindful when engaging in any activity.

- **Mindfulness helps make your mind blank and calm:** A lot of old-school meditation practices are centered around "silencing" your thoughts and emotions, but that's not what mindfulness is about. With mindfulness, your intention is simply to acknowledge and welcome every part of your human experience in the moment.

- **Mindfulness is the same as concentration:** The intention of mindfulness is not to concentrate on one thing in particular, but to remain present in whatever task you're undertaking, whether that's eating, driving, doing your work, or tending to your children and pets. As you get used to practicing it in your everyday life, you'll get better at staying in this mindful space.

Benefits of Mindfulness

Distractions and stress are at an all-time high. Between work, social media, family issues, and friendships, it's becoming increasingly difficult for us to stay in the moment. Luckily, mindfulness can be your awareness bestie. Modern research has shown that integrating mindfulness into your daily routine can have a positive impact on your mental, physical, and social well-being, even within a few weeks.

For one, being more mindful can help you boost your positive emotions because you won't be dwelling on the past as much, preventing you from feeling stressed or anxious. And as we all know, decreased feelings of stress or anxiety aid in better and deeper sleep, which then leads to a healthier immune system over time. Mindfulness as an immune system booster is backed by research as well![5] Even as a certified workplace mindfulness instructor, I have to remind myself to keep up with my personal practice on a daily basis to reap these benefits.

As my thirties creeped on out of the picture, my memory began to slowly shimmy along with them. Let me tell you how real it got. One day, I was walking around my condo, turning it upside down in search of my house keys only for me to finally take a seat at my kitchen table and realize my keys were in my hand the entire time. Chile, the embarrassment of it all. When I began diligently practicing my moment-by-moment awareness, the mindful juices started to flow more freely and I haven't had an incident like that since. In a 2020 study done at University of the

Sunshine Coast, researchers found that mindfulness helps rewire parts of your brain to support healthy aging, increased productivity, decreased stress, and stronger memory.

Let's have a sidebar nerdy moment about the brain because, quite frankly, I find it interesting that something that seems so simple and practical, like mindfulness, can have such a major impact on helping my brain function optimally.

Neuroplasticity is your brain's capacity to change, heal, or adapt its neural pathways, which helps support your overall health and function. Harvard researchers did a study back in 2011 that revealed that a consistent mindfulness practice can positively impact the function of your hippocampus, which supports learning and memory and can fight dementia. This same study also saw a decrease in the size of the amygdala, the fight-or-flight VIP lounge where our stress, anxiety, and fear tend to hang out.[6] A smaller amygdala is correlated with lower stress and anxiety levels. I support all of this! I mean, forget eye creams and retinoids, I need to keep my mindfulness up in my medicine cabinet of self-care practices.

I have a deep and personal relationship with my mindfulness practice. If I'm being honest, it has been my saving grace in many high-conflict scenarios, from dealing with irate melanin-deficient team members during performance reviews to driving in that good ol' DMV Beltway traffic during my daily commutes. Chile, I enjoy the occasional glass of wine like everyone else after a tough day, but using mindfulness as a coping mechanism is way healthier than developing a drinking habit. Am I right? I don't know who this is for, but showing people what them hands do is so 1998. We've elevated to "May the Lord watch between me and thee," and "Per my last email . . . ," and graceful "nice nasty" readings for filth in this era of Black excellence. I know, I get it. A little bit of "mess around and find out" finds itself in my spirit every now and then too, but using mindfulness as an emotional regulation tool has been a godsend.

Now, don't get me wrong, we're not in the business of allowing people to take advantage of us, and I'm definitely not asking you to ignore real-life scenarios that might truly require a more aggressive response. Instead, I am sharing that mindfulness is a tool that can help you take a mental beat before you act. This moment of pause gives you space to respond gracefully based on the truth of the scenario versus knucking and bucking at every Karen, Ken, or Kesha who rubs you the wrong way.

I will warn you now: this practice is not anger-proof. You are still human, after all. You're not going to wake up every day beaming sunshine on Gullah Gullah Island; however, consistently practicing mindfulness will help you feel more grounded and in control of the moment.

Ten years ago, I had no idea what the heck mindfulness was, but now, in my late thirties, it's become a normal part of my routine like brushing my teeth. My hope is that you don't see mindfulness as another item on your massive to-do list or just another strategy for self-improvement. Instead, think of it as grace's little cousin. It's less about *doing* and more about *being*. If you take on this mindset, I'm certain mindfulness will become one of your new self-care besties.

Practicing Mindfulness

Let's say someone cuts you off in traffic. Your first thought might be, *This mutha***** just cut me off! Now, I'm pissed.* And guess what happens next? You immediately start to embody the feeling of being pissed off. In that moment, there is no buffer between the thing that pissed you off and your reaction to it. You might want to catch that person at the next red light to give them a fist sandwich, or you might settle for a quick bird flip if you're in a hurry.

Okay, now let's add a pinch of mindfulness to the mix. If someone cuts you off in traffic, you can instead inhale for three seconds and exhale for three seconds. Then take notice of how you're feeling. In this example, maybe your face is hot and your heart is pounding. Once you've acknowledged those sensations, go back to your breath, inhaling and exhaling for a count of three. Then, try to see if you can identify any other sensations. Maybe your shoulders are tense or your hands are gripping the steering wheel. Repeat this process of breathing and noticing for a few moments, and you'll find that when you see the person who cut you off at the red light, you'll be less likely to turn the situation into an episode of *Love & Hip Hop*.

Another mindfulness practice I rely on is the simple body scan. This is something you can do to start your day, to decompress after a stressful meeting, or even to relax when you see that no one in the house has washed a dish, knife, or fork after you've cooked. Let's practice the body scan for this next chapter challenge.

CHAPTER CHALLENGE

This body scan is my gift to you so you can become acquainted with what you are feeling at this moment. This is a great way to check in with yourself without judgment. Before you begin, remember to check in with your mindfulness guidelines:

- No expectations
- No judgment
- Be an observer
- Have a beginner's mind

When you're ready, review the following body scan steps so you can complete this practice uninterrupted. The goal here is not perfection. Follow these instructions as best as you can and do what feels right when you're unsure of what comes next.

1. Lie down or sit comfortably in a chair.
2. Take a few deep breaths, inhaling through your nose and exhaling out your mouth.
3. Bring attention to your physical body and how it feels in the bed or chair.
4. Take time to notice each of your body parts, starting from the top of your head and going all the way down to your feet.

Slowly acknowledge each body part, pausing when you feel the need to.

5. Perhaps you may need to relax your jaw and other facial muscles or unfurl your brows.

6. Roll your shoulders up, around, and down your back, then allow them to relax completely.

7. Continue down your body until you reach your toes and every muscle is relaxed.

8. Notice how things feel without judging or trying to change them.

9. When you're done, take two deep breaths then open your eyes.

GROW TIP: A body scan is a great practice to try right before a big meeting or an important conversation. Tapping into your physical body in this way helps you get centered and brings a sense of calmness into an otherwise anxious or stressful moment.

By identifying and challenging the irrational beliefs that influence your behaviors with the power of the ABC model and incorporating a consistent mindfulness practice into your daily routine, you'll have personal access to a transformative approach to overcome negative thoughts, destructive behaviors, and hurdles blocking you from experiencing greater well-being in all areas of your life.

With these techniques, you'll gain more insight into what makes your mind tick so you can replace the negative patterns keeping you from being your best self. However, remember that it is mindfulness that takes this process to a deeper level. Mindfulness, with its ability to help you experience moment-to-moment awareness and nonjudgmental acceptance, teaches you to observe your thoughts and feelings without getting distracted by them. Being more mindful allows you to navigate your daily life with more patience, acceptance, and compassion. By incorporating mindfulness into the practice of the ABC model, you can cultivate higher levels of self-awareness and master your emotions and reactions.

Aligning both of these growth tools will help you break free from the shackles of negativity, empowering you to overcome self-destructive habits, cultivate more optimism, improve your overall well-being, and lead a more profound, joyful, and fulfilling life.

Now that you know how to maintain your mind over your mind chatter, join me in the next chapter, where we'll talk about an essential well-being practice that will transform your relationship with yourself and other people: setting boundaries.

CHAPTER 5

DRAW THE LINE

Rescuing Your Time and Peace of Mind with Boundaries

C lick*

Oop! My momma just hung up the phone on me in mid-sentence. RUDE! Needless to say, we were in the middle of a not-so-favorable conversation where I disagreed with her perspective and *respectfully* made her aware of my opposing perspective. I emphasize the word *respectfully* here because 1) my momma is Black, 2) she didn't raise a fool, and 3) I'm grown, but I don't want those kinds of problems.

If I'm being honest, though, this kind of communication was consistent with prior disagreements. Growing up, I believed this kind of behavior was normal. As a child, it felt like we just had to suck up our opinions and feelings to "honor thy parents." After all, there was no gentle parenting campaign going around for my parents to take advantage of. Growing up southern and Black for many of us meant many of our parents held the belief that children should be seen and not heard. The slightest thing—from voicing an opinion or having a rebuttal to not wanting to go to church or wash dishes—was considered disrespectful "back talk." The idea of you, the child, having an opposing perspective, opinion, or even an ounce of feedback to give your parents was treated as one of the greatest offenses of all time. So when my mom hung up on me that day, I was disappointed, but I wasn't at all surprised.

Now, let me be very clear: this is not an indictment on my mom. Viewing this through a more mature and empathetic lens, I realize human beings are multifaceted and that also includes the people who raised us. Regardless of my gripes with some of her behaviors, my mother is *that woman*. She raised four children as a single parent and worked multiple jobs to make sure we had everything we needed. There are so many qualities and characteristics that make her a phenomenal and resilient woman, and today, we often laugh at how much of a drill sergeant she was back in the day.

Oftentimes in the Black community, our parents either created their parenting style from scratch or mimicked what they saw as children. Knowing this after my exposure to positive psychology, I was able to have a bit more grace with my mom during this conversation. From my new perspective, I knew that if I wanted change in my relationship with her, I would need to initiate it. I would have to set the boundary. Typically, my reaction would have been to let the incident fly until she decided to call me back days later. But at this point I had resolved within myself that I wanted to teach people how to treat me and this included those closest to me. Yes, even my mother.

In my small-group coaching circles for women, one of the most critical topics we cover before we even blink at goal setting is reviewing and confirming areas of their well-being that feel a bit unbalanced. Most of the time, their challenges are due to a lack of clear boundaries with the people who occupy those spaces. After a few sessions of walking them through this process, I realized I had to turn my coaching tools on myself to figure out where I was lacking as well. I couldn't be a hypocrite. I had to do my own work. I needed to create a communication boundary with my mother in hopes that it would create more opportunities for us to connect more freely and with mutual love and respect.

So, I did not call her back that day. She more than likely wouldn't have answered the phone anyway. Instead, I decided to send a well-crafted text message (because I'm a millennial) so my new boundary could be set in writing. I sent her a text message that read something like this:

> Hey Ma, I did not expect you to hang up on me in the middle of our conversation. I feel disappointed with how this conversation ended today. I make it a point to be respectful to you, even in my most heightened moments. I do not raise my voice, cuss you out, or hang up the phone because you raised me better than that. At 30-something years old, I would like to receive the same kind of respect that I give to everyone else, regardless of the relationship. In order for us to have respectful and productive communication, please refrain from hanging up the phone in the middle of a disagreement. You would want me to give you that level of respect, and I think I'm owed the same.

Whew, the audacity on my part, right? I know. Trust me, I was afraid. I still have an ounce of residual fear of my mom from childhood (you know how it is), but I knew this step was necessary for my peace of mind and for better communication in our relationship. I took what I'd been learning in my months of positive psychology training and set a real-life boundary. This was HUGE! I imagined myself receiving a standing ovation of appreciation and approval from my thirteen-year-old self.

It's one thing to set boundaries with coworkers or clients, but taking this approach with my mother was a whole other thing, and it gave me a boost of confidence and pride I didn't realize I needed.

If this incident with my mom had happened in my early twenties, it would have gone down totally differently. She would have ignored me for a few days (activating event), I would think to myself, *She is never going to change; this is just the way it is* (belief), then I would have been silently resentful and cut our next phone conversation short. We both would have acted like nothing happened, and I would feel unresolved in my spirit (consequence).

I began to recognize this type of behavior on my part was not productive and didn't leave me feeling too hot. I didn't feel like I was honoring the growth I'd worked so hard on. I had learned new ways of navigating relationships and new rules for engaging in communication with the people around me. I knew if I continued to allow this to fester, the consequence would be detrimental to the woman I was becoming. The boundary was mandatory for my continued transformation journey. It's tough, uncomfortable work, but the reward (peace of mind) is always worth it in the end.

Think of your transformation journey like you would losing weight. Reframing your limiting beliefs and shifting your mindset will yield changes within you, but making a lasting change requires discipline, consistency, and healthy boundaries.

The *Oxford Dictionary* defines a physical boundary as "a line that marks the limits of an area." Your personal boundaries, though not physical, operate the same way. In her book, *Set Boundaries, Find Peace*, therapist Nedra Tawwab describes personal boundaries as "expectations and needs that help you feel safe and comfortable in your relationships." I like to think of boundaries as an open invitation to lovingly teach people how to treat you and respect your personal space. This is a technique that would have been so helpful for me as a Black woman coming into her own after relocating to a major city.

In a conversation with one of my closest friends who works as a therapist for teens and young adults, we talked about our upbringing and our parents' reactions to these "new age" emotional tools. We both laughed as she recalled a time her mom had a visceral reaction anytime my friend said the word *boundary*. I could totally relate. People in my life have had similar reactions, and I attribute this to their perception that you are attacking their character. But most of the time, a personal boundary is being set to protect and honor the person's experience in that relationship or connection.

I acknowledge that boundaries can be a touchy subject for some, especially if you've always been someone people go to for help and support. You may even be feeling hesitant to set them in your life. Before you run off and decide boundaries are not for you, let's debunk three common myths about their purpose.[1]

- **Myth #1: Boundaries hurt relationships.** The truth is, setting boundaries with the people we love can be very intimidating and even scary. Many people will ignore their own needs out of fear because they don't want to lose the relationship or upset someone. In actuality, setting healthy boundaries can help us communicate more effectively with our loved ones while creating space to deepen the relationship.

- **Myth #2: Boundaries are one-size-fits-all.** The truth is, all boundaries are not created equal. Experts recommend you set boundaries that are flexible and unique to each relationship. This will allow you to preserve the connection while honoring your needs.

- **Myth #3: Setting boundaries results in big, dramatic blowups.** The truth is, you can practice setting healthy boundaries that are subtle, soft, or even invisible to the people they apply to. A soft or invisible boundary might look like not immediately replying to text messages or putting your phone on Do Not Disturb before bed. The intention of a soft boundary is to give you agency and power without the other person's knowledge.

Now, you might be thinking to yourself, *Oh no, I'm good. I don't have a problem with telling people what I think or getting folks together.* Or maybe you're the complete opposite and you're thinking, *How do I even know if I need to set a boundary?* Either way, I got you! Our good sis Nedra Tawwab shares a few tell-tale signs that you might want to consider checking in on your imaginary fences, even if you feel you're already doing so:

- You feel overwhelmed.

- You feel resentful toward people who ask you for help.

- You avoid phone calls and interactions with people who might ask for something.

- You often make comments about helping people and getting nothing in return.

- You feel burned out.

- You frequently daydream about dropping everything and disappearing.

- You have no time for yourself.

Now, everybody turn to your neighbor and say, "Neighbor, you need some boundaries!" I've seen pretty much every one of these signs within the women I coach who feel like their homes and schedules are out of control. What I've discovered from working primarily with Black women is that we often try to do everything and we are slow to ask for support from the people in our lives. That right there is not sustainable, nor does it honor your mental, emotional, and physical well-being.

The benefits of setting boundaries far outweigh the misconceptions. Boundaries truly add value to your well-being goals because you can count on them to enhance your sense of autonomy and help you avoid burnout. By creating clear boundaries as a way to protect yourself and show up better for other people, you will start to:

- Have more meaningful friendships and relationships

- Feel less stressed

- Communicate more clearly and with more intention

- See more availability in your schedule

- Trust the people you care about more

- Use "no" more frequently and confidently

As scary as they may be to set, boundaries are a great way to express love and care for ourselves, and they allow us to decide how we navigate our connections, which helps us create more authentic and fulfilling relationships. With this in mind, let's spend some time breaking down the different types of boundaries that can support you as you relate and respond to the people in your life.

Mental boundaries give you the freedom to honor your values and perspectives on how you want to show up and express yourself in the world. For example, let's say a close friend has offered you unsolicited advice on how you should have reacted to a conflict at work. They believe you should have been more aggressive in your meeting with your current manager, but you feel your approach was appropriate. Setting your boundary could sound like, "Thank you for sharing your work experiences with me. I respect your perspective on career development, but I don't agree with your approach. I know what works for me."

Emotional boundaries help you manage how emotionally available you are in relation to the people around you. So, if a coworker calls you every day to vent about their marriage problems, but you find you just don't have the bandwidth to hear it this time, you could set a boundary by saying, "I really want to support you during this challenging time, but this week is a tough week for me, and I do not have the emotional capacity to hold space for you."

Material boundaries help guide your finances when it comes to loaning or giving to people. Let's say you have a cousin who has consistently asked to borrow money while you try to save up for a new phone. In this case, you could set a boundary by saying, "I've let you borrow money for the past few weeks, so I won't be able to lend you anything else for the next couple of months."

Internal boundaries help you manage the energy you exert for yourself in comparison to what you exert for others. For example, let's say your group of girlfriends is going out for bottomless Bellinis for the third consecutive weekend, but you've noticed you've started to lag behind on your to-do lists because of the weekend shenanigans. As much as it pains you to turn them down and miss out on the fun, you know you need to prioritize yourself and set a boundary. You could say something like, "As much as I love y'all, I've been social and spending money in these streets all month, so I'm going to use this weekend to catch up with life."

Conversation boundaries relate to your comfort level of discussing certain topics. Let's say you have a very well-intentioned but nosy neighbor who notices that your partner hasn't visited for the last week or so. She sashays over as you're checking the mailbox and inquires about their whereabouts. You're not super close to this lady and would rather not tell her all your business, so you say something like, "I would rather not discuss what's going on in my household. Thank you for respecting my privacy."

Physical boundaries help you manage your privacy and personal space. I'm sure many of us have no problem setting these boundaries, especially nowadays as we've become more aware of transmissible illnesses, but for those of you who like examples, consider this: You're in the grocery store checkout line and a random person walks up to introduce themselves to you. She recognizes you from a mutual friend's Facebook profile and shares that she loves the cute pictures you post of your toddler. She reaches down to hug your child, which prompts you to then say, "Thank you for your kindness, but please don't hug my daughter. I don't allow people she doesn't know in her personal space."

Time boundaries help you navigate your calendar and availability. Most people believe they have a time management issue, but the truth is that many of us have a problem with setting boundaries around our schedules. For example, let's say you get invited to a game night with Black Card Revoked, Taboo, and Spades on the menu, but you know you have to get up in the morning for a boot camp you just committed to. To set this boundary, you could say, "Thanks for the invitation. I'd love to join you; however, I'll only be able to stay until 8:30 pm because I have a workout class in the morning."

All right, now that we have a solid understanding of what boundaries are and what each kind looks like, it's important that we focus on constructing clear and effective ones. In general, a clear and effective boundary should:

- Have well-defined and decisive limits, but also remain reasonable and flexible

- Prioritize your needs as well as the needs of others

- Focus on your authenticity rather than victimhood or people pleasing

- Help you channel emotions, such as anger and frustration, in a constructive way rather than turning aggressive or shutting down

- Be rooted in reality, focusing on what the situation actually is instead of what you or others want it to be

If you're hoping to experience all the positive changes of doing the work around self-awareness, happiness, emotional regulation, and positive thinking, it is important that you prioritize your needs first and foremost. Setting boundaries can be intimidating and sometimes extremely scary, especially when you're still building confidence in yourself. My hope is that you use this knowledge to build and maintain a healthier relationship with yourself and the people in your life.

CHAPTER CHALLENGE

As we close out this chapter on boundaries, I would love to do a boundary life audit with you. This will help you practice leveraging your "no" so you can create more space to say "yes" in your life. There is no reason you should feel like an extra in your own story. Let's cultivate that main character energy!

The Invitation: This challenge has two parts. Set a five-minute timer for each.

Part 1

Write and consider your thoughts and feelings using the following prompts for each area of well-being (social, financial, physical, community/spiritual, career).

- In each area of well-being, list everything that helps you feel secure, cared for, and appreciated.

- In each area of well-being, list everything that makes you feel insecure, unsupported, and unappreciated. Put a star beside the items that are within your control.

Part 2

This next part is called "Hell Yes or Hell No," adapted from psychologist Robert Shuster's "Hell Yes" rule for productivity. This exercise is a client favorite that helps you put things into perspective and set limits that honor your happiness. Clients have said this process helps them feel empowered and able to talk about their sh*t in a healthy and productive way.

Step 1

Think of all your current commitments, both business and personal, and in your journal, put them into one of three columns—Hell Yes, No (For Now), or Maybe.

Step 2

1. **Go through the Maybe column** and clear it out completely. Do what you need to do to turn these items into a Hell Yes or a No (For Now).

2. Now that the Maybe column is empty, **scan the Hell Yes column** and pause here. Does it feel overwhelming to make these commitments? If so, you're not alone. This is often the case for women who wear many hats within their family and friend groups. Which items could you move from the Hell Yes column to the No (For Now) column? Start by moving items that drain you of your energy.

3. **Scan all of your No (For Now)** items and apply each to one of the following three categories: Revisit in three months, Revisit in six months, Revisit next year. This part of the exercise allows you to keep track of things you want to remember to do. You want to get these done, but you realize that later in the year just makes more sense with your current obligations.

Becoming a master boundary setter helps you safeguard your physical, mental, and emotional well-being, with your boundaries serving as security guards for your sanity that help you protect your energy and prioritize your personal time and needs. By getting clear on your boundaries, you are telling yourself and those around you that you are worthy of a life filled with ease and respect.

You've done a lot of self-inquiry over the last few chapters, and I think you deserve a break. Remember, this journey we're on together is not about getting to the finish line quickly. Take your time digesting and savoring the process. As we wind down here, do something kind for yourself. Grab a hot cup of tea, take a walk, call a friend, or meditate. I'll be here when you get back, okay? See you soon!

CHAPTER 6

TAKE CARE

Using Self-Care as a Pathway
for Healing and Restoration

Welcome back! I hope you took advantage of my recommended grace break after chapter 5. If you are making the time to work through these practices with me, you've totally deserved it. Now that you have a solid foundation for setting clear boundaries, I want to shift your attention to explore how self-care can be a helper for healing and restoration.

My intention is not to put you on the therapy couch; instead, my hope is that you can feel the transformative power in incorporating small but impactful care practices into your daily routine. I wish I had the late-night commercial prescription drug announcer voice on right now that would say, "Please note that the details provided in this chapter are not a substitute for professional medical or psychological advice or treatment and are not intended to diagnose or treat any mental disorders as defined by the American Psychiatric Association. As the reader of this book, it's your responsibility to seek independent professional guidance if needed. If you are currently receiving treatment from a mental health professional, I encourage you to let them know you're reading my book. Maybe they can use it as supplemental support for their other clients."

So listen, I recognize that self-care and healing are both trending topics within the collective consciousness of millennials and Generation Z. But there's more to self-care than taking bubble baths and getting massages. It's equally, if not more, vital to unlearn what people have taught you about yourself. I am grateful to exist in a time where the conversations around Blackness and womanhood have shifted from presentation and performance to truthfulness and authenticity; this is where true self-care lies.

Summer in the Washington, DC, area feels like a warm and loving hug from Afrobeats Drake and pineapple mimosas. It's literally one of my favorite times of the year. If you've spent any time here, then you know the number one pastime of the Black and brown girls across the Beltway is, you guessed it, brunch! I believe brunch was sent down to us from rich auntie heaven so all of us could enjoy the pleasures of delicious comfort food, flavorful libations, and a dope playlist of good vibrations. Plus, it's during the day, so it's like a fun night on the town without the guilt of being out too late on a school night. By far, my favorite thing about brunch is the many conversations I have with my girlfriends on the topics of healing, therapy, and happiness. Of course, most of these intense conversations take place after a second round of bottomless fruity libations, but they are legitimately profound, and the gems dropped are limitless!

The recurring themes in these lively small group talks include everything under the sun: limiting beliefs, confidence and self-esteem challenges, being underpaid as Black women in every industry, Black Jesus, white Jesus, Michelle Obama's hair, social media trends, working out, the dating pool having pee in it, and finally the idea of being the "strong Black woman." *Ugh, can we let her go home and rest, please?* Brunch with the girls feels like talk therapy without the productive interventions. There, we can sit together and dissect every aspect of our lives. Black Girl Brunch is sacred.

Since I can't recreate many of the enlightening moments I've had over mimosas, I decided to bring a glimpse of my inner circle to you. I sent out the following voice note because, yes, I am *that* friend who loves herself a thoughtful voice note to get their point across. Here is a glimpse of what a few of my friends had to say in response. All of the names have been changed to protect the privacy of my crew.

My Invitation and Question to The Crew:

> We know that for many Black folks, healing appears to be seen as a "luxury" or something we don't have the time to think about, but knowing you as a member of my inner circle, I understand that it's something that's important to you. If you had to think about a moment that shifted your approach to self-care and healing, what would it be? What gave you the "nerve" to do something about it?

The Crew's Responses:

> July 2014. I was unemployed, had no idea what I really wanted to do in my life, and just ended what I thought was a serious relationship. At that moment, I realized that "space" was toxic for me because everything I did in it was based on what society told me was "successful." I decided to heal by setting myself free of all those standards and leaving the safety net. I started from scratch so I can write the story with my own ideas, so I can at least look back and say I did it my way. This was my way of healing . . . most thought I was crazy, and many said they could never do it, but I refused to hold their fears.
>
> Dawn, Brooklyn, NY

> What gave me the nerve to heal was being reminded of who I had forgotten myself to be. A mentor had to literally show me my why through a self-inventory exercise . . . he also held me accountable to lots of spiritual study and sent me tons of inspirational messages that he asked me

to journal and reflect on. My proximity to his spiritual maturity and frequent encouragement made it DIFFICULT to stay in my "dark place."

Lisa, Baltimore, MD

In order to live an authentic life and make deep and meaningful connections, I had to show up as my full self and that included being vulnerable with the risk of getting hurt. And to no longer allow any form of fear in any domain of my life to drive any of my decisions.

Jamie, Athens, GA

My best friend was tired of hearing me talk about the same things/men's issues. I did not realize I was going in circles until she told me she could no longer help me and I may need to speak to a therapist. That was the jolt I needed. I thought I had it all together, but after hearing someone I trusted say I might need more help, it gave me a wakeup call. Once in therapy I started to see how essential it was, and it opened my eyes to all the areas I needed to heal.

Jean, Stafford, VA

I am grateful to my friends for being willing to share their truths with me. Their responses prove that healing and restoration can take on many different forms. I appreciate that each of their journeys started with a moment of awareness followed by intentional action toward their own versions of freedom. Giving yourself permission to heal and following through with intentional action is no small feat. What would your life look like if you gave yourself permission to heal?

The strong Black woman stereotype has perpetuated the unrealistic idea that women who look like us are damn near superhuman. As a result, many of us are NOT okay; Black women around the world are suffering from exhaustion, overcompensation, insecurity, trust issues, and anxiety due to this archetype. Should we be celebrated for being pillars of fortitude, love, and protection for our families, friends, and extended community? Absolutely. The flipside is we've spent more time leaning into being these glorified pillars without the respect and emotional support required to carry it all.

When I was younger, my mom would close her door and climb into her bed after work every day. I just assumed she was tired and this was something that all grown-ups did. As I got older, I recognized that her behaviors were signs of depression, and her way of coping was to isolate and regroup. Along the same lines, I remember visiting my grandmother during the holidays and noticing a table full of medications. One day while we were watching *The Andy Griffith Show*, I got curious and asked her which medications were for what. She went through the whole table. For some of them, she couldn't even remember why or when she started taking them. The one container that stood out to me was what she called her *nerve pills*, which I now understand to be her anxiety medicine. I know for sure my mom and grandmother's stories aren't unique. I've had many conversations with clients and friends who shared their stories and desires to break this cycle of trying to have it all together all the time.

The truth is we cannot fully blame the people around us. There is power in taking accountability for your own emotional health and healing. For far too long, we have smothered our sadness with busyness, hiding our hurt through performance and presenting a happy face through the pain. When left unchecked, these feelings can manifest into pain and disease in the body. But I am hopeful. In a few post-COVID conversations with clients and colleagues, I've noticed a shift toward ease and rest.

If no one has said it to you yet, then let me be the first to tell you to GET OFF THE STAGE. I say this with love. It is time to stop performing and presenting in a way that is detrimental to your mental, physical, and emotional health. We should do a collective unsubscribe from any habit or behavior from the *Strong Black Woman* newsletter. Do we have to completely disregard the parts of ourselves that get sh*t done? No. Instead, my invitation is for you to become an alchemist of your self-care. This level of mastery requires you to be truthful about your needs and commitments to yourself and other people, understand how to get these needs met, and create authentic self-care practices that support your restoration.

I believe self-care is a revolutionary practice. When I am coaching my clients around their care regimen, I'm not telling them to go on an expensive vacation or book a spa day. (No shade to the spa, I love it there!) This external type of self-care is equally important, but the problem is that in mainstream media, external self-care is all that gets highlighted. Now, before you get your panties in a bunch, I understand that self-care rituals are different for every person. Full disclosure: going to the hair salon is part of my self-care package, but I also know when to dig deeper in my toolkit to restore my energy and soul from the inside out.

So what is self-care, really? A more recent, research-based definition of self-care is "the ability to care for oneself through awareness, self-control, and self-reliance in order to achieve, maintain, or promote optimal health and well-being."[1] Low-key, high-key, self-care sounds a little bit like Jesus. Seriously, reading that definition gives off that Philippians 4:13 energy. Just jokes. God knows my heart. So now that we're aligned on an updated definition of self-care, let's tackle a few self-care myths for the folks who might be struggling with it or are new to the self-care squad.

- **Myth #1: Self-care is selfish:** The truth is, resting and recharging is one of the healthiest and thoughtful things you can do to show up for yourself and those around you.

- **Myth #2: The effects of self-care are temporary:** The truth is, self-care is more than short-term pleasure and relaxation. The key is to find out what recharges your energy more than something like a bubble bath.

- **Myth #3: Self-care is just for women:** The truth is, we all experience inner and outer stressors. Anyone can benefit from a self-care routine.

- **Myth #4: Self-care takes too much time:** The truth is, self-care can be easily mapped into your busy day. Treat it like any other activity that you schedule into your calendar, so it feels like a regular part of your day.

- **Myth #5: Self-care is doing anything that soothes you:** The truth is, self-care should promote and support your well-being, and anything that is addictive or harmful to your body should not be a part of your routine, even if it temporarily soothes you.

- **Myth #6: Self-care is the same for everyone:** The truth is, we all have different stressors and ways of handling them. The way self-care looks will be different for each individual person. What you need to recharge and feel in control might be completely different from what makes me feel ready to take on the world.

Raise your hand if you've made any of these excuses before? If you raised your hand in real life, we're probably made from the same pot of gumbo. I support having fun when no one is watching.

GRATITUDE AS A FORM OF SELF-CARE

Before I dig into how to design your custom self-care toolkit, I want to talk through two of my go-to self-care practices for myself and my coaching clients, starting with gratitude. One of the first life lessons many of us learned from our Black grandmothers was the idea of counting your blessings. For generations, Black folks have turned to the practice of gratitude as a source of strength and resilience in the face of adversity.

The wisdom passed down by the matriarchs of our families has not only carried us through years of oppression and patriarchy, but it's also globally backed by research as a strategy to increase life satisfaction and resilience. In "Counting Blessings Versus Burdens: An Experimental Investigation of Gratitude and Subjective Well-Being in Daily Life," a study completed by Robert Emmons, professor of psychology at University of California Davis, and experimental psychologist Michael E. McCullough, suggests that practicing gratitude makes us happier and boosts our overall well-being. Gratitude is like a secret sauce for accessing joy. Not only does it improve our mental well-being by reducing feelings of depression and anxiety, but it also strengthens our social connections and helps us do a better job of nurturing these relationships. This is so important because it's often much easier to focus on the negative traits of the people closest to us; however, when we choose to focus on their positive attributes instead, it keeps us open to finding common ground. Practicing gratitude even has an impact on our physical health by improving our sleep patterns, boosting our energy levels, and enhancing our overall vitality. So, when we think about self-care, it makes sense to incorporate gratitude into our daily lives as an essential practice. It's the magical ingredient that takes care of our mind, heart, and body, helping us thrive in every aspect of our lives.

I'm impressed by the number of studies that speak to how vital gratitude is as an asset on this journey toward transformation. In her book, *The How of Happiness*, Sonja Lyubomirsky explains the significance of gratitude as a way to take care of our mental and emotional well-being. She shows us that gratitude isn't just some fluffy idea; it's a powerful habit to redirect our mind when we're in need of an upward spiral. And you know what happens when we do that? We shift our focus to the good things in life, and it becomes a magical elixir that brings us contentment, joy, and inner peace. It's such a simple act of self-care that can have a tremendous impact on our well-being.

What's fly is that Lyubomirsky's book also shares how gratitude can be beneficial in the day-to-day navigation of personal growth, helping us uncover hidden gems that have the potential to make a real difference in how we nurture our well-being and find inner balance.

So what exactly is gratitude and how do we practice it? Well, first off, it's all about savoring the good stuff and appreciating the lesson in every moment, even the seemingly insignificant or challenging ones. Relishing in those small experiences can help maximize our satisfaction and enjoyment in life. But that's not all! Gratitude also boosts our self-worth and self-esteem. When we take time to appreciate our wins and acknowledge the dope things our loved ones and higher power do for us, it's like a confidence boost on steroids. We find that it's easier to value ourselves and the people around us even more, and I love that for us!

Hey, and when life gets tough, and it will, gratitude becomes a healthy way to cope with our challenges. Being grateful in the face of adversity helps us adjust, heal, and move forward. It's like hitting the reset button and starting fresh. Oh, and let's not forget about the comparison bug. We all know that comparison is the thief of joy, but gratitude shuts that down faster than a new color release from Telfar (Yes, I'm still trying to get that green screen shopping bag!). When we're genuinely grateful for what we have, we stop obsessing over what Joseph, Tom, or Caresha have. Instead, we are more focused on our own blessings. Last but not least, gratitude kicks negativity to the curb. Seriously, it's like the ultimate mood booster. When we practice gratitude, negative emotions like bitterness, greed, anger, and jealousy just can't stick around. It's hard to feel resentful when you're feeling grateful, you know what I'm saying?

CHAPTER CHECK-IN

Before we learn about my other self-care practice faves, let's pause here for a quick gratitude check-in. Grab something to write on and answer the following questions:

- What are you grateful for at this moment?

- What is one thing about yourself you are most proud of?

- Who's a family member you've now come to appreciate?

- What are you grateful for now that you used to take for granted?

- Look at your cell phone and write out the names of three people who have reached out to you in the last week and schedule a time to do the same for them.

It's such a game changer to see how something as simple as counting our blessings and practicing gratitude can have such a profound impact on our well-being. Now, let's shift our focus to another aspect of self-care that may seem a little unconventional at first, but carries tremendous significance as we think about how to better care for ourselves: forgiveness.

FORGIVENESS AS A FORM OF SELF-CARE

You know, forgiveness is a tricky thing. I want to say up front that forgiveness doesn't mean we have to forget what happened or let someone off the hook for their actions. There's a big difference between forgiving to let go of our pain and "forgiving" just to make the other person feel better. It's all about prioritizing our healing and releasing the burden that's been weighing us down.

Now, here's a tip for those struggling to figure out this distinction, especially when dealing with manipulative individuals. First, trust your instincts and listen to your emotions. Manipulative people often twist the idea of forgiveness to serve their own agenda and avoid taking responsibility, so it's important to prioritize your well-being and protect yourself from further harm. Don't hesitate to lean on your trusted friends, family, or professionals for support and guidance. They'll be able to help you see through the complexity of the situation and move forward in the way that's best for you.

Lastly, let's acknowledge that some things are simply unforgivable, and that's okay. Not everything deserves to be or can be forgiven. In those cases, it's best to focus on forgiving yourself for holding onto that pain for so long. Embrace self-compassion and understanding, allowing yourself to heal and grow, even without extending forgiveness to others.

All in all, forgiveness is a personal journey, and there's no one-size-fits-all approach. Take care of yourself, honor your feelings, and find your own path to healing and peace.

For a long time, I was the CEO of Blame It on the Rain Incorporated. Take ownership? It's always *their* fault, right? "Their" being my mom and dad. I blamed my father for not being around for the majority of my formative years. It's his fault that I didn't get to be a daddy's girl. I blamed both him and my mother for not creating a loving environment because if they had, maybe I would have sought love and acceptance from inside my home, right? And when my twenties came rushing fast, after graduating from college and moving to a big city where my friends and I were having hot girl summers before there was a label for it, they were the reason I engaged in toxic friendships and relationships. (This is the point in the book where the old Southern Saints are clutching their pearls at the transparency. How dare I tell my business to the world? I'm sorry, but like Deacon Carter said, I can't heal what I don't reveal.)

I clearly needed to take ownership of my own actions, which was a concept I learned early on from my therapist, who had me journal answers to the following questions: "What role did I play in creating the problem?" "How can I accept responsibility for my own actions?" "Who would benefit from an apology from the part I played in the problem?" "If I hadn't contributed to the problem, what will it look like to build a bridge forward with this person? What resources can I lean on? Who can help me build this bridge?" I used these questions to build a bridge with my own dad who I didn't have any form of a relationship with for years. After talking to my therapist about our non-existent relationship, she told me to think about what role I played in this issue. At first I was like, WHAT YOU MEAN, I didn't ask to be abandoned! But after digging a bit deeper, she asked what was stopping me from at least *trying* to have a new, possibly different relationship with him as an adult. The only answer I could provide was my years of feeling hurt and disappointed with him for not being around. At this big age, though, I had the ability to call him myself and get the answers to the questions I'd been wanting to ask him. I realized I'd been the one avoiding phone calls and not stopping in to visit him when I was home from DC. As an adult, I was contributing to the distance while claiming I wanted to rebuild the connection. I decided to build a bridge and invite him to coffee after my thirtieth birthday. I asked all the questions I needed to ask and told him everything that was on my mind. He not only received it, but he also apologized. Today, I wouldn't say we're super close, but we have a very cordial and respectful relationship.

Many of us are unknowingly operating from hurt and unhealed places, and taking ownership is the first step toward taking your power back. Even now, when I'm faced with conflict, I ask myself: *What role did I play in the outcome of this?* Listen, more than likely, I might have had a small part to play in the misunderstanding. We grow. We learn.

When I started owning my behaviors and my role in situations, it opened up space for forgiveness, which is, in my opinion, the most important pathway to healing. And not just any regular-level forgiveness. I mean a deeper level of forgiveness, of myself first and then other people. Traditional forgiveness tends to focus on seeking peace within yourself and letting go of the negative emotions without losing sight of what happened to you. This deeper level of forgiveness that I'd been pursuing, and that I took one step further with my parents, meant that I was not only seeking peace within myself and working on letting go of the negative feelings, but I also saw it as an opportunity to look at them through a different lens. I considered who they might have been in their twenties and thirties, thought about the childhood pain and traumas they both might need to heal from, and started to view them with more empathy and compassion. This gave me the wisdom and insight to start viewing everyone in my life this way. My unwillingness to forgive was hurting me. The pain I carried in my heart was impacting my relationships and friendships. It impacted my ability to trust and genuinely love. Some of us truly believe that holding a grudge will "show them" (our alleged offender) a thing or two. Chiiiile, let's be real: you ain't showing them anything but how hurt people hurt people. So how do we move forward? Well, before I tell you how to move forward with forgiveness, let me tell you why you should consider it in the first place.

- People who are forgiving are less likely to be "depressed, hostile, anxious, angry, and neurotic"[2] and are more likely to be happier, healthier, and more serene.

- Practicing forgiveness helps you let go of the desire to change the past and move the heck on quicker and with peace.

- Practicing forgiveness decreases negative rumination about a particular event. Instead of sulking and stewing in your feelings about something that happened, you can acknowledge that it was an event in your life, figure out what you learned from it, and do what? Move on!

- Practicing forgiveness helps us let go of feelings of resentment, regret, and revenge, which are all HEAVY emotions that promote being stuck. And guess who doesn't have time for stagnation? WE DON'T.

- Practicing forgiveness helps move you out of a narrow and focused state into a "broaden and build" state.[3] It opens your mind, heart, and arms, giving you the opportunity to receive whatever the universe is ready to pour into you.

I know you may be saying to yourself, *I don't have a problem with this. I just forget it ever happened and move the heck on.* No, ma'am. That's not what I'm talking about. Forgiving is NOT the same as forgetting. Forgiving is a GIFT that you give yourself of not allowing what he did, what she didn't do, or what happened to you when you were little to plague your mind and take over your life. Forgiveness gives you freedom. Don't you want to be free?!

You may be saying, *Well, Chianti, all right. I get it. Forgiveness is something I probably should be working on, but where do I start?* I'm so glad you asked. The first thing you want to do before you even think about forgiving anyone else is to take inventory of yourself. What are some things that you haven't forgiven YOURSELF for? What are some things that continuously vex you and make you believe that you don't deserve what you have? Write each thing down in your journal. Next, close your eyes, take three deep breaths, and open your eyes. Beside each "offense" write down "I am forgiven for X because I deserve to be free." Take as much time as you need to do this, and when you finish, close your eyes again and repeat these words to yourself: "I am forgiven for all of these things because I deserve to be free." The goal is to believe it with all of your heart because you deserve to be free.

Now that we've taken care of you, let's talk about forgiving other people. Identify at least one person whom you have been holding an offense against. Write their name down on a piece of paper. Close your eyes and picture yourself in a dialogue with this person. Imagine that you all have decided to meet for dinner or coffee or even just at your home. Imagine yourself extending grace to this person for mistreating you or offending you. Try to empathize with them and view the situation through their eyes. Imagine seeing them as a whole person—a flawed human being like everyone else. Imagine yourself granting this person forgiveness. Think about the words you need to say and the grace you need to extend, then take three final deep breaths and let . . . it . . . go.

There is this dope book I like to read that says, "For if you forgive men when they sin against you, your heavenly Father will also forgive you" (Matthew 6:14-15). It's the WISDOM for me!

CREATING YOUR OWN SELF-CARE TOOLKIT

Next on our agenda, let's circle back to the benefits and types of intentional self-care because I like to know the why behind anything I do. Self-care is truly something that supports you in any phase of life, so it's a good idea to understand the full picture of the resources that are available.

Can I share another moment of transparency with you? Life be life-ing, even for me as a trained and certified coach in positive psychology. During my program, the best part for me was not only the interventions and practices but having a classmate coach me through how to apply them to my life in real-time. I often tap into this stash of practices on a consistent basis because burnout, stress, and overwhelm do not discriminate, not even for those of us who focus on supporting and caring for others.

The most powerful form of self-care is proactive care. What does being proactive look like in real life? Well, it might look like creating and updating your very own self-care toolkit, an intentional set of daily or weekly rituals that help you nurture and restore your five areas of well-being, both internally and externally. Because we all lead different lives and have unique mental, emotional, and physical needs, your self-care toolkit might look different from mine.

This self-care toolkit should aim to restore your energy, inspire rest and ease, spark joy, and replenish your mind, body, and spirit. As you change and grow, so will this toolkit. The key is to customize it to honor every area of your life and update it for every season you endure. If you need more convincing on why you should create a toolkit for yourself, here are a few additional benefits to having one:

- **Improves your personal relationships:** When you feel like your best self, you're better able to care for and show up for the people you love.

- **Enhances your mental health and well-being:** Practices that focus on connecting with people trains your mind and helps release feel-good hormones like oxytocin and endorphins.

- **Manages your stress and anxiety:** Practicing self-care activates your parasympathetic nervous system, which slows down your heart rate and breathing, allowing you to relax your mind and body.

- **Prevents illness:** Taking care of your mind and body helps reduce the chance of developing health conditions like stroke and heart disease.

- **Maximizes your productivity:** Consistently practicing self-care helps improve your cognitive abilities, which unlocks better focus and concentration.

CHAPTER CHALLENGE

If your natural instinct is to give, give, and give some more, this is a friendly call-out for you to start paying more attention to your care regimen. Small changes to your self-care can have a major impact. I think you've gotten enough context around the importance and benefits of having your own customized self-care toolkit, so now it's time for a check-in.

The Invitation: Go back to the previous chapter's check-in and refer to the well-being areas where you noted feeling insecure, unsupported, and unappreciated. From that list, review the items you placed a star beside and answer the following:

- **Current Tactics:** What tactics are you currently using to remedy the personal and professional commitments you highlighted? Include your current self-care tactics as well as your not-so-productive strategies to cope with stress. There is no judgment here. This is simply an opportunity for you to get a clear look at what you need to add to your custom self-care plan to feel more secure, supported, and appreciated in specific areas of well-being.

  For example:

    ◦ Midday naps

    ◦ Early morning workouts at least four times a week

    ◦ Check-in walks with friends

    ◦ A glass of wine to decompress after a stressful day

- **Current Self-Care Needs:** Make a list of your current needs from the five areas of well-being. For practice, you can just start with two needs for one area.

  For example: Social Well-Being

    ◦ I want to feel connected. I spend a lot of time alone.

    ◦ I want to feel heard. I spend a lot of my time lending a listening ear, but rarely feel like this is reciprocated.

- **Practices That Support Your Needs:** Make a list of self-care activities that will support the needs you listed above. Consider activities that bring you energy, joy, or calmness.

  For example: Social Well-Being

    ◦ I want to feel connected. I am currently feeling lonely.

    ◦ Self-Care Ideas: Join a ministry at church this month, invite two friends over for Girls' Night In on Friday, create of list of friends to reconnect with and schedule a check-in walk with each by the end of the week.

- **Sustainability:** Be gentle with yourself. The best path to success with a new self-care plan begins with small changes and simple strategies. Try adding one thing at a time to your schedule based on what logistically makes sense to do daily, weekly, and monthly.

For example:

- April Self-Care Toolkit for Social and Physical Well-Being

  - First Wednesday: Attend Singles Ministry Bible study and social hour

  - Thursday Evenings: Schedule one check-in walk with a different friend each week

- May Self-Care Toolkit for Social, Physical, and Financial Well-Being

  - First Wednesday: Attend Singles Ministry Bible study and social hour

  - Friday Evenings: Host a movie night for two of my friends, and ask each of them to reciprocate the following weeks

  - Saturday Mornings: Restart my weekly money meetings to review my personal expenses, bills, and debt progress, and update my Mo' Money Playlist to make it fun

Before we close this chapter on care and restoration, I'd love to make a quick pit stop at the intersection of self-care and professional care as it pertains to healing and support. In my training to become a positive psychology-centered coach, one of the first concepts we learned was Dr. John Travis's Illness-Wellness Continuum. This continuum describes various phases of health at two opposite ends, focusing on building your well-being through emotional regulation, increasing holistic awareness of your health, and taking ownership of your current state.[4]

Life can throw you all kinds of challenges that impact your state of being, so you might find yourself at different points in the continuum. One key point I want to share is that within the continuum, the presence of wellness does not indicate the absence of illness, nor does one side of the continuum represent success or failure. Human health and well-being are a lot more complex than that.

I use this variation of the continuum as a self-help tool for myself and my clients to identify what type of support (i.e., self-care practices and/or professional help) is needed at any given moment. My particular method of coaching focuses on helping women move north of neutral. When you find yourself on the left side of neutral, you might want to consider therapy. I have recommended therapy over coaching for a few potential clients because in that season of healing a licensed mental health expert would be more effective in getting them back to neutral. This self-help tool is just another way to better understand ourselves, tap into our internal needs, and welcome more healing and restoration into our lives.

If you're unsure if therapy is right for you, here are a few signs it might be time to seek support from a professional.[5]

- You feel hopeless.
- You have irregular sleep habits.

- You're feeling more overwhelmed than usual.

- You tend to avoid social situations.

- You have a hard time controlling your emotions.

- You have intrusive thoughts due to extreme stress or anxiety.

- You don't care about life.

- You struggle with emotional eating.

- You've experienced traumatic events, like abuse, addiction, or abandonment.

- You're experiencing extended grief.

By the way, every therapist I've had has been a Black woman. I can't bear the thought of having to give context for the Black experience every time I tell a story like, "Oh yeah, she SAID she was going to knock me into next week, but she really didn't mean it that way." Honestly and truly that's not even possible; however, the threat of it was enough to get you straightened out by a parental figure. If you immediately thought to yourself, *I don't have the budget for a therapist,* know that I understand completely. I remember when I was newer to the search process and I had no idea where to start. Here are few things to consider when trying to find the best fit for you.

- Where should I look?

    - Psychology Today: Online directory of therapists. Using filters like Issues, Insurance, Gender, Types of Therapy (there are so many options in this one, but my personal favorites are CBT, Positive Psychology, and Psychodynamics), and, of course, Ethnicity Served will get you the best results.

    - Open Path Psychotherapy Collective: A nonprofit organization that provides affordable online and in-office psychotherapy options.

- Talk Space: Online, personalized 24/7 therapist-matching service.

- Better Help: Online convenient and affordable therapist-matching service.

- What questions should I ask?
  - Are you licensed in my state?
  - Do you currently take my insurance?
  - What kind of experience do you have with someone who has my concerns?
  - What kind of therapy treatments do you specialize in?
  - What fees do you have for missed sessions?

There are so many additional questions you could ask, but those should get you started. My recommendation is to treat this process as carefully and intentionally as you would when you're finding a primary care provider. You're trusting this person with your most valuable resource: your mind.

By practicing self-care and embracing therapy, you are providing yourself with the kindness, care, and love required to be more resilient. As you face different seasons in your life, there will always be a desire for meaning and purpose. In this upcoming chapter, we are going to look into how faith and spirituality are sources of truth for many of us who believe in something or someone bigger than ourselves.

CHAPTER 7

NO CHURCH IN THE WILD

Finding Meaning Outside of the Pew

I want to test the vibe real quick. When I say, "God is good." You say? And when I follow up with, "And all the time?" You say? If you were able to complete those responses with ease, you, my dear, might be a little Black churchy, or at least come from a churchy Black family.

Look at us, my churchy friend! We've made it one step closer to creating a life that is energizing and supportive. (Sidebar: Even if you don't go to church, I'm sure you've heard that from someone's great auntie or uncle.) I want to acknowledge you for taking an active role in your personal transformation. More specifically, I want to celebrate what you've done up until this point around building your awareness, defining your version of happiness, unpacking limiting belief systems, setting boundaries, and curating a self-care toolkit to refill your cup. You may have learned some things about yourself that you didn't expect, and after the last chapter, you may have uncovered new things that can fill your cup.

For me, that unexpected cup-filling activity was yoga. When I finally decided to try it, I jumped all the way out of the window, bringing my close friend Tomkins with me to try a hot yoga class. It felt like the perfect combination of mental and physical support to help me decompress from tons of traveling I was doing for work at the time. As Tomkins and I explored the local yoga communities, they were giving *Dawson's Creek* energy and I really needed *A Different World*. I wanted yoga, but with a little more soul.

I was living in northern Virginia at the time, so finding somewhere to practice with Black and brown faces was not an easy task. Then one day I discovered a Black woman-owned yoga studio within walking distance of my apartment. How Sway? I guess when the yogi is ready, the studio will appear. My classes were led by phenomenal Black and brown women who made me feel welcome and safe. My favorite class to attend on Tuesday evenings was called My Body Don't Bend That Way. When my instructor, a beautiful Black woman with locs wrapped in an Erykah Badu-style headwrap, closed out our practice with "I Am Light" from my girl India Arie followed by affirming words of love, joy, and kindness, I knew I had found my people.

Before we continue this conversation on spirituality and the church, I have to acknowledge the historical importance the Black church has played in the progression and growth of Black people in America. For more than two hundred years, the Black church has been a sacred and safe space for Black folks across the diaspora. Church was a place where our grandparents and maybe even parents went to have transparent meetings on social justice issues, prepare themselves for leadership roles, or safely socialize away from the watchful eye of Jim Crow. For me and many of us in my generation, we went to church because we had to; it wasn't really a choice. If you stayed out all Saturday night at the teen club or skating rink, guess what, Momma Lomax expected you to be up bright and early to catch the church van.

You see, I grew up in the Blackity Black church, a "run around the sanctuary five times, cover your lap with a napkin if you're a woman sitting in the front row, starting your Sunday at 8 am for Sunday school and staying at church until 4 pm for afternoon services" kinda church. Listen, to this day, when the choir lets off "Total Praise" or "Excellent," you better step aside because I might just take a lap or two around the sanctuary myself!

I, like most young adults, went through a lot of transition. I had to navigate some really difficult emotions and life experiences on my own. I felt disconnected. I wasn't grounded in anything. If you've ever relocated from a small city to a larger one you might understand where I'm coming from. Even with a host of friends, you can still miss home. Instead of driving down Augusta Road to Washington Street to get to Grandma Georgia Mae's couch for a bowl of greens and cornbread, I had to drive down I-95 to I-85 and cross a few state lines. Home was now an eight-hour drive away. After a while, it became a little tough to reckon with.

So I started looking for the one thing that always worked: a church. One Sunday morning, my sorority sister talked me into visiting this prominent, historically Black Baptist church with a conservative feel. I wasn't completely blown away by the traditional-style worship service, but the sermons by their new, younger pastor from the South Side of Chicago felt customized for the exact mental and spiritual season I was in at the time: responsibly ratchet with a hint of righteousness. I decided to stop dating other churches and landed on this one that felt most in alignment with my growth. I was so thirsty for connection and belonging that I signed up for all the ministries—young adult, outreach, prayer, social media—and I even did some TV anchor spots for the media ministry. I was immersed in everything at the church, just trying to feel more connected to myself and other people. If "doing the most" was a person, it would be me with a fresh twist-out and some pearls.

If you grew up anything like I did, then you know that church was the solution for everything. Feeling sad? Go to church. Marriage on the rocks? Go to church. Can't find a job? Pay your tithes anyway, and go to church. Sadly, I got to a place where Sunday service just wasn't enough for my blues. Something important was missing. For a while, I would dress up on Sundays, make my way to the church house, and upon arrival, I would walk to my favorite seat close to the pulpit. On one side would sit a deacon's wife or any other beautiful sister who was dressed to the nines. People would ask how I was, but, trust, they didn't really want to know. What they wanted to hear was, "I'm blessed and highly favored." No real connection. But I can't look down on them because I was trained to do the same thing: keep my business to myself.

When I moved to the DMV, I thought I was living my best Black life. I had a new job, my salary wasn't too shabby, I eventually moved out of my cousin's house and found my own apartment, and I started my Sunday brunch ritual with my friends. From the outside looking in, I was thriving, but on the inside looking out, I didn't feel like I was on solid ground. I couldn't figure out why I felt so disconnected from myself. Can you relate? Everyone else believes your life is on track, but little do they know that internally, the building is on fire, you are out of water, and there is nowhere to turn. Whew, chile, I am not about that life. Well, at least not anymore.

Growing up in a Black church, many Elders believed that anything that was not directly mentioned in the Bible was the devil's work. We were told to pray the stress away, and I can't even lie: I internalized it for myself. As a result, I looked at yoga from afar for *years*, but ultimately decided to steer clear of anything that didn't look like traditional Baptist behavior. This misconception that other spiritual practices and my Christian principles could not coexist was crippling, which goes back to the importance of our thoughts and beliefs.

I had an outdated belief system around spiritual practices that originated outside of my churchy upbringing, and those beliefs informed my decisions and life experiences. After the skydive jump I told you about in the introduction, I chose to face my fears head on and lean into my curiosity. My positive psychology program was the catalyst for it all, allowing me to connect the dots between spirituality, religion, meaning, and purpose in a more practical way.

A moment of clarity that stands out to me the most was when I learned the difference between religion and spirituality. There isn't an extreme difference between the two, but there is a clear distinction in how they are executed in daily practice. For years, I just assumed they meant the same thing, rolling my eyes to the back of my head anytime someone would say, "Oh, I'm not religious, I'm spiritual." I just assumed most of the people who said it did not understand what it meant either.

The National Alliance of Mental Illness describes religion as "an organized, community-based system of beliefs," while spirituality resides within the individual and what they personally believe. There is spirituality within religion, but if you are spiritual, it doesn't necessarily mean you are religious too. My internal aha moment came when I realized both religion and spirituality were instruments I could use for my overall well-being. It's sort of like finding out an old friend is a fraternal twin. Like, how didn't I know that after all these years? So now, when people tell me they are spiritual, I totally get it.

Religion traditionally has focused on community, structure and predictability, and teachings from a sacred text or deity. On the other hand, spirituality has been linked to individuality, acceptance of everyone regardless of religious affiliation, and the ability to shape one's own practice. What I've found is that the benefits to your overall well-being converge from a positive psychology perspective. Rather than defining your faith as religious or spiritual, positive psychology allows you to use both experiences to create a foundation in something bigger than yourself, teaching you compassion, forgiveness, and gratitude, empowering you to cope with stress in healthier ways, and inspiring awareness of your impact on the world.

Growing up as a Black Southern Baptist, the concepts of spirituality and religion seemed so distant in how they both functioned as anchors of meaning and positive growth. I know now that spirituality already exists within monotheistic religious structures and functions as your personal faith experience, allowing you to connect deeply and authentically to what you already believe in. The purpose of this chapter is not to convince you of anything other than to consider if any preconceived notions or outdated belief systems are preventing you from having a more divine connection within your human experience.

I'd been actively practicing my religion since I was around nine years old, and I realized it was time to step outside of my comfort zone and explore my relationship with spirituality. Positive psychology has been the gift that keeps on giving in that regard. Because of my exposure to all of the research and adjacent mindfulness and neuroscience communities, it's been almost eight years since I was introduced to the benefits of the now-mainstream practices, like gratitude, self-compassion, and mindfulness meditation. These practices weren't as trendy when I was going through my program, at least not among my circle of Black women. I still remember my path of discovery.

Mindfulness meditation introduced me to yoga, which took me down a path to Yoga Teacher Training, which introduced me to the Sutras and Asanas, which made me realize how much ancient texts like the Bible, the Qur'an, and the Vedas are rooted in similar principles, such as the law of reciprocity, truthfulness, virtues, and forgiveness. My perspective on faith and spirituality broadened exponentially. If you are curious about how you might go on your own spiritual journey outside of traditional, conservative religious structures, my advice is to shift how you view it. Think of spirituality as personal development for your faith. Once you change your view of how spirituality can contribute to your growth and well-being, start by asking God or whoever you pray to for guidance, wisdom, and an open heart for the journey. Next, I would set an intention. Think about what you want to learn. What are you curious about? Be open to what comes up for you, and try not to judge yourself if these interests fall outside of cultural norms. Finally, I would use your intuition and logic to seek out spiritual mentors and communities that feel safe.

This chapter is not a call for you to escape the church (or any organized religion), but it is an open invitation for you to explore spirituality with fresh eyes and get curious about what it means for you in your personal self-care and transformation journey. Younger generations of Black folks across the US are now having way more nontraditional but impactful and healing faith-based community experiences that offer a chance for them to develop real relationships with God and their fellow worshippers. It may not look like a brick-and-mortar building on the corner, but it's spiritual healing all the same.

Matthew 18:20 says, "Where two or three are gathered in my name, I am there." This verse has taken on a whole new meaning for me, and I am grateful for this new understanding. God is truly good. Now that my own spiritual practice includes both a life of prayer and mindfulness meditation, it's up and it's stuck! Baybeeee, Jesus gets my BEST prayer life when I'm centered and at peace. This is what mindfulness provides for me. It gives me the emotional space to not just pray for myself but for other people in my life. I get to truly love my neighbor the same way I love myself because I've taken the time to learn how to *actually* love myself. I know Jesus was pleased when I made space for my faith, spirituality, and religion to coexist.

CHAPTER CHALLENGE

I stand firm in my belief in Jesus Christ as the son of God. I still pray, attend church in person, and even tune into Bedside Baptist Church a few times a month. However, my spiritual life is more like gumbo now: I started with a base of Jesus, added daily mindfulness and journaling, four ounces of yoga, two scoops of affirmations by Londrelle and Toni Jones, and now I'm out here levitating through these streets.

Okay, I've spent a lot of time in this chapter sharing my spiritual walk, but now the time has come for you to check in with yourself. So, what's in your pot?

The Invitation: In your journal, reflect on the following prompts:

- Has your perspective on religion and spirituality changed since you were a child? If so, how?

- What limiting beliefs do you need to call out that might be holding you back from exploring the spiritual practices that interest you?

- What spiritual practices are you hoping to bring into your daily life?

- What five spiritual practices keep you grounded? (Example: Bible devotional, journaling, morning yoga, inspirational music playlist, meditation)

I want to close out this chapter by sharing that I love awakening to new things because it allows me to see the potential of what's in front of me. Reframing how I view religion and spirituality has given me the creative license to support, love, and care for myself fully and without limitations. It feels like freedom. I still thoroughly enjoy a good in-person worship service because fellowship with the Saints is ingrained in the fabric of how I praise God. I don't see that changing anytime soon, but the difference now is that my spirituality is not confined to an institution or a building. My spirituality is humanity. It is compassion, integrity, and honesty. It is generosity, which is what inspired the outpouring of content you're reading now.

CHAPTER 8

BREAKING BAD

Upgrading Your Habits to Boost Your Well-Being

My typical morning starts like this: If it's a workout day, I get up, brush my teeth, throw on my workout clothes, and then make my way to the gym. When I get home, I shower and then start my morning routine. On days when I don't hit the gym, as soon as I wake up, I head straight to the bathroom to freshen up. Brushing my teeth is my first order of business. There's something about the minty-fresh, clean feeling that instantly wakes me. After that, I wash my face and moisturize because Black don't crack, but it does dry out a little.

Back in my room, I grab my journal and cell phone, fluff up my pillows, and get back into bed for a spiritual tune-up. First, I open the Bible app on my phone to read the scripture of the day. Then, I have a little talk with JC about the happenings in my life, even though he is already fully up to speed with the shenanigans. Once I'm done with the Bible app, I reach for my gratitude journal to jot down three things I'm grateful for at that moment, which helps prepare my mind for the day ahead. After expressing my gratitude, I write down three things that would make my day amazing, which helps me anchor my day on what I want to accomplish the most. When I'm done journaling, I make my bed. A few years ago, I read a book by Admiral William H. McRaven, named *Make Your Bed: Little Things That Can Change Your Life . . . and Maybe Even the World*, and it really struck a chord with me. No matter how messy my room may be, I make it a point to make my bed every morning. It's a small act, but it gives me a sense of order and accomplishment.

After my spiritual check-in, I head to the kitchen to fix my morning tonic. It's a simple concoction of warm water, turmeric, freshly squeezed lemon, and a pinch of cayenne pepper. Now I'm going to be honest with you friend, it doesn't taste the best, but it helps jump-start my digestive system, which helps boost my metabolism for the day and tames my issues with bloating. The ladies over thirty-five get it!

With my tonic sipped and my body ready to do its job, I treat myself to a cup of coffee with a splash of almond milk. Armed with my caffeine boost, I do a quick standing yoga stretch and grab my laptop to make a to-do list for the day, jotting down the tasks I need to complete and seeing which meetings I can push off to the next day. This helps me stay organized and ensures that I tackle the important stuff.

My morning ritual is made up of habits that help prime my thoughts and body for the day. This topic is specifically important to me because I live by the old adage of "We are what we repeatedly do." If we truly want to flourish in this next season of life, the best place to start is with an examination of our habits. For the rest of this chapter, I want us to take time to look into the science of habits. I've referenced habits earlier in the book, but it's important that we take a closer look at the rituals and routines that can make or break our ability to grow and thrive.

We often talk about habits haphazardly in our day-to-day lives, usually discussing the ones we know we need to change but struggle to move the needle on. But before we move deeper into the chapter, I want us to get aligned on a general definition. A habit is a personal practice or routine you consistently complete that is either intentional or unintentional.

WHERE DO HABITS COME FROM?

From a scientific perspective, habits are created in our brain via a four-step feedback loop that James Clear, author of the book *Atomic Habits*, calls the "habit loop."[1] This habit loop is his own adaptation from the super popular book *The Power of Habit* by Charles Duhigg. This four-step loop includes a cue, a craving, a response, and finally a reward. The cue is like a little signal that tells your brain to start a particular behavior. Cues are often things you see, hear, or feel, and they help your brain predict a reward. For example, a cue could be walking down the street and smelling pizza, hearing your phone ring, or simply waking up in the morning.

Next comes the craving. A craving is the motivational force behind every habit. Cravings happen because we desire a change in how we feel inside, not necessarily because of the habit itself. We all have different cravings because they're influenced by our thoughts, feelings, and emotions. Once you have the cue and the craving, the response kicks in, which is the actual habit you do. For instance, when I wake up in the morning (cue), I crave to feel alert, so my response is to go to the bathroom to wash my face and brush my teeth. And finally, there's the reward, which in this case is feeling alert and refreshed. Now, whether or not you actually do the habit depends on how motivated you are and how much effort it takes. The brain loves the easy way out, so if something feels too hard or you're not motivated enough, you'll find the habit harder to stick with. This is often why we find it challenging to correct some of our most ingrained habits; it's much easier for our brains to do what they've always done.

But here's the dope part about all of this: when you complete the habit, you get a reward, which satisfies your cravings and ultimately makes you feel good. A reward can be as simple as feeling relieved or content, and it teaches your brain which actions are worth doing in the future. So, rewards operate like tiny reminders that this habit is something you should continue to do.

The catch is, though, in order for a behavior to become a habit, all four steps need to be present: the cue, the craving, the response, and the reward. If any of these steps are missing, the habit ain't going to stick. The big warning sign that I want to plaster on this loop is that it applies to intentional, healthy habits AND unproductive or bad habits that you weren't even trying to create. For example, let's say you're working on presentations and emails at home (cue). You feel stressed and overwhelmed by the work, so you crave to feel more in control. As a response, you grab a big bowl of barbecue chips and proceed to eat the entire thing. The reward is that you satisfy your craving to reduce stress, so over time, your brain associates eating chips with working from home.

This is why mindfulness and self-awareness are key in your growth journey. Being aware of why you do what you do and when allows you to run your habits instead of allowing them to run you. Mastering the art of creating a habit gives you more autonomy to build ones that are doable and consciously transform your entire life because as we know: *we are what we repeatedly do.*

MAKING AND BREAKING HABITS

What's great about the habit loop is that it can be repurposed as a simple behavior change framework to create productive habits that will add value to your life and get rid of unnecessary behaviors that no longer serve you. The steps from the habit process serve as a set of rules to change human behavior. When they are aligned correctly, forming healthy habits feels natural and easy, but when they're in the wrong positions or missing altogether, it can be really tough to stick to the habits you desire. When you are wanting to create a productive habit:

1. Make the cue or trigger for your habit really obvious. You want it to stand out so you can't miss it.

2. Make your habit attractive. Find ways to make it appealing and enjoyable so you're motivated to stick with it.

3. Make the habit easy by breaking it down into small, manageable steps. The easier it is, the more likely you'll do it.

4. Make the habit satisfying. You want to feel good or get some kind of reward from completing the habit. This is what makes it stick!

Now, if you want to break an undesirable habit, you can flip these rules around. Instead of making the cue obvious, make it invisible. The intention you're aiming for is to remove any reminders or triggers that lead to the bad habit. Out of sight, out of mind! Next, instead of making the habit attractive, make it unattractive. Find ways to link negative consequences with the habit so it loses its appeal. Then, instead of making it easy, make the habit challenging to access. This is when I give you permission to be a hater. Introduce obstacles or blockers that make it harder for you to engage in this unproductive habit. For example, I've been training myself to have focused work time without scrolling through social media, so I often turn my phone off or leave it in my bedroom so it takes more energy to access it. Lastly, make the habit undesirable. Take away any rewards or benefits you used to get from the habit.

I want to be clear here: these four rules of behavior change aren't the only way to transform your habits, but they are practical and basic enough that you can apply them to any habit you wish to develop.

CHAPTER CHECK-IN

Take a moment to think about that annoying habit you've been itching to break, one that's been holding you back from reaching a personal goal or milestone. Maybe it's the habit of hitting the snooze button one too many times in the morning, indulging in late-night snacking, or doom scrolling on your phone when you should be finalizing a project. Next, focus on a habit you would like to create in its place. Use the rules of human behavior and the habit loop to help you design your plan.

The Invitation: Grab your favorite notebook or open a fresh document on your computer. Let's knock out a game plan to take this habit down! This is your chance to get up close and personal with your behaviors and design a strategy that fits your unique style and circumstances. Are you ready? Let's get into it! In your journal, work through the following prompts.

Breaking a Bad Habit

- Write down a habit you would like to get rid of sooner than later. Capture the cue, craving, response, and reward for this habit.

- How can you place this habit out of sight and out of mind? What reminders or triggers do you need to remove?

- How can you make it undesirable? What can you do to link negative consequences with the habit so it loses its appeal?

- How can you make the habit challenging? What obstacles or blockers can you put in place?

- How can you make it less satisfying?

Creating a Good Habit

- What habit would you like to create in its place?

- How can you make it more visible? What reminders do you need?

- How would you make it attractive?

- How would you make it easy?

- How would you make it satisfying?

Your habits can make or break your journey toward optimal well-being. The goal here isn't to be perfect; instead, it's to recognize the ways we are intentionally or unintentionally holding ourselves back from being the best person we can be. I hope you revisit this exercise whenever you become aware of a habit that you either want to break or build to set yourself up for success in your daily routine. In the next chapter, we'll discuss visualization and its role on our pathway to intuitive goal-setting.

CHAPTER 9

DREAMS UNLOCKED

Casting the Vision and Setting Intuitive Goals

Well, this suitcase ain't gon' pack itself.

There I was again sitting on the edge of my bed on the verge of tears, dreading my weekly commute to Jersey City. Not only was I working on fumes from a lack of sleep, but I had a check-in the next morning with one of the most toxic managers I ever had in my entire career. After working through a severe case of the Sunday Scaries (shout-out to my cousin for letting me know there was an actual term for this feeling), I turned on my Robert Glasper playlist and grabbed my journal for a bedtime reset.

With "Afro Blue" playing in the background, I took a deep inhale and exhale, then answered the question "What would my ideal workday look like?" I vaguely remember writing something like,

> I gently wake up in my own bed to the sound of birds chirping. I write out my gratitude and hopes for the day in my journal. I follow this up with my morning bathroom routine. I make a healthy breakfast and sit down at

my dining room table to eat and have coffee. By the way, I work remotely from the comfort of my own home. I'm excited about the workday because we're kicking off a new health initiative for our team. I log into my laptop around 9:30 am to check my schedule and emails. At 11:00 am, I have my first meeting with my team. We laugh and joke together about the shenanigans of the prior day and cocreate a plan of attack that benefits the clients' needs and our company. After my midday yoga practice, I log back onto my laptop for my bi-weekly check-in with my boss. We talk about our shared love of podcasts and our top three shows at the moment. She asks me about my roses and thorns of the week and then we discuss how she can better support my development over the coming months. I have my last client meeting around 3:30 pm. I do a final scan of my email for the afternoon and log off. I toss on my sweatpants and sneakers and head outside for my afternoon stroll.

Seven months later, I found myself working at a 100 percent remote tech company whose company culture was centered around the greater good of their clients and the well-being of their workforce. A testament to the power of visualization.

The process of changing into the person you would like to become requires you to set productive goals, track your progress, and achieve what you set out to do, which are all skills that must be learned and cultivated. At this point in the book, you are probably experiencing one of two things: crazy gratitude for the abundance of self-care and growth practices you now have available to you or a deep sense of overwhelm as you realize how much work lies ahead. If you're on the latter side of things, here is my invitation to you: be patient with yourself. There is no urgency to do all the things at once. You have the power to implement as many or as little of these practices as needed. Learning how to set and achieve attainable goals will help you manage the stress and overwhelm that comes with making major life shifts. We will delve into the details of how that works in just a moment, but first, let's leap headfirst into one of the foundational components of goal-setting: visualization.

Visualization is a practice that involves focusing on positive mental images to motivate you toward achieving a specific goal. This technique can be a groundbreaking tool that helps you bring your dreams to life, helping you anchor your goals, create excitement around them, open your mind to new possibilities, and boost your self-efficacy (belief within yourself) to take the next best steps toward achievement.

There are two methods of visualization: process visualization or outcome visualization.[1] Process visualization is imagining yourself taking the steps and actions that lead you to your desired outcome. With this method, the goal is to envision the what, how, and when while engaging all of your senses. This method works to inspire you to take immediate next steps while creating an emotional connection to the goal that lies ahead. Outcome visualization is imagining yourself at the finish line of your goal with no specific details on how you get there. The visualization I shared in the beginning of the chapter was an example of outcome visualization. I dropped right into describing what it would be like if I had the job of my dreams without having a plan of attack for how to get there. Combining these two types of visualizations is a super boost to your goal-setting process.

CHAPTER CHECK-IN

When coaching my individual clients and small groups, we begin our goal-setting journey with the end in mind, so you know what time it is. It's time for a chapter check-in! I want you to get some practice with this as well.

The Invitation: Take three deep cleansing breaths, inhaling through your nose and exhaling through your mouth. After the third cleansing breath, read over the following scenarios, then write everything that comes to mind in your journal. Don't edit yourself; instead, allow your thoughts to lead you.

Visualize Your 365

Part 1: Imagine it's 365 days from today, and you're looking back over the past year with amazement at everything you have been able to achieve. What phenomenal things have taken place to make you feel this proud? Consider the type of person you've grown into. What do you look like physically? How are your energy levels? What healthy habits and attributes have you adopted?

> **GROW TIP (OPTIONAL):** If you need a bit more structure with this, feel free to reference your areas of well-being to list your victories. Give your mind permission to roam free. There are no obligations or commitments. Turn on a good playlist with inspiring tunes and let the energy flow.

Part 2: When you're done, glance over your notes, then close your journal. Take one deep cleansing breath (inhale through your nose, exhale out your mouth) and close your eyes. Envision what you wrote down in your mind's eye. Remember, the more detailed and specific you are, the more impactful the visualization will be.

For the folks who might be thinking, *Chile, this visualization stuff doesn't work for me,* or if you have actual challenges with this based on a personal condition, you can try one of the following alternatives. As you read over what you wrote, try to tune into the senses and emotions of what it would be like to accomplish those goals or be in those places. For extra credit, try reading your notes out loud. Notice how you feel as you do so. If you're feeling creative, grab your art supplies (markers, scissors, glue, old magazines, etc.) and spend some time creating a visual collage of what you wrote in your notes. Create a mini vision board on a blank page in your journal that presents a visual translation of your thoughts. Personally, I love a good vision board. I've kept all of the ones I've created over the years. These are not the perfect equivalents to visualization, but you will experience the same cognitive benefits you would as if you were completing a visualization exercise.

This visualization check-in is a fan favorite because imagining the wins prepares your mind and body for success and can boost your confidence and overall belief that they are possible. When I've tried to help clients set goals without completing this practice first, there was a clear difference in their mindset and energy. Their goals seemed unattainable to them, perhaps even too far-fetched to truly invest their time and energy to accomplish. But clients who start with the visualization practice tend to display a more positive disposition, and you can tell right away that they feel empowered. I always start those visualization sessions by telling my clients that we're about to take restrictions off their goals to allow their minds to wander.

PRIMER FOR GOAL SETTING

Now, what I'm about to say about goal setting might be a little different from the traditional career coaches and goal-setting fanatics. Instead of leaning on a structure like SMART goals, I've adopted a more intuitive approach to goal setting in hopes of bringing in fresh energy around setting my intentions for the year. As an avid goal-setter and self-help connoisseur, I've tried every goal-setting method under the sun, and I've found the most success with this intuitive approach. I found that visualization and a primer around my emotions helps connect me to my goals on a soul level, and this method has worked the same for my clients. This primer for goal setting starts with more internal reflection (yep, we're going there again). Instead of going in hot, writing down goals and aspirations, first ask yourself, "How do I want to feel?"

Consider the visualization you just completed and the prior year or even the last couple of months and decide what feelings would honor the highest version of yourself, the version of you that upholds your values and has attributes that would empower you to lead a more intentional, focused, mindful, and grounded life. For the folks who are traditional "top of the year" goal setters, you can add specific timeframes to these questions: "How do I want to feel by the end of the year?" or "How do I want to feel within the next six months?" If you want to take it one step further and tune into your whole self, you can inquire about the feelings you'd like to have within each area of well-being.

GROW TIP: Creating an annual ritual around intention or goal setting helps trigger new habits, build your self-confidence, create inner accountability, and provide a way to measure your progress.

Let's walk through an example together. Pretend it's January 1 of a new year and you are doing your annual goal-setting session with this new intuitive approach. The first thing you need to do is map out your five areas of well-being on a dry erase board or a blank piece of paper. Now, ask yourself, "How do I want to feel by the end of this year or in the next six months?"

- **Career:** *I want to feel accomplished.*
- **Community/Spirituality:** *I want to feel connected.*
- **Financial:** *I want to feel secure.*
- **Physical:** *I want to feel light and energized.*
- **Social:** *I want to feel loved and cared for.*

Set Your Goals: Big Juicy Goals (Long-Term)

Once you've completed this list of statements, translate these statements into goals. What big juicy goals would you need to accomplish to manifest this feeling? Big juicy goals are typically long-term milestones you'd like to reach within six months, one year, or three years that help define what success looks like for you. These types of goals will require more effort and time to achieve. For example:

- **Financial:** I want to feel secure.

  Goal: *Save more money for an emergency fund.*

- **Physical:** I want to feel light and energized.

  Goal: *Adopt a sustainable plant-based diet.*

> **PRO TIP:** Prioritize your long-term goals. If you have a list of ten or more long-term goals, select the top three you want to focus on during a specific time period (six months to one year from now).

Break Down Your Goals: Bite-Sized (Short-Term)

My coaching clients are all intelligent, loving, hardworking, creative, and ambitious women with gigantic dreams. They have a vision for acquiring generational wealth and healing their familial traumas, but they come to me because they feel overwhelmed, underappreciated, and in need of support while juggling their many responsibilities, including their personal goals. This is where I step in. My secret sauce to making sure goals are achieved is by breaking them down into bite-sized chunks. I know you are thrilled to create so much magic over the coming months with your long-term goals; however, I want to make sure you're coming out of the gate with a strong blueprint for reaching them in a way that promotes ease and not exhaustion. The most prevalent difference between long-term and short-term goals is the time and effort it takes to complete them.

To create an overwhelm-resistant goal plan, start by reviewing your long-term goals and prioritizing your top three. Next, take time to cut those three goals down into smaller, actionable, and measurable short-term goals that move you closer to your desired outcome. The goal here is to break down your massive milestone goals into tiny, digestible pieces that can be achieved now or in the very near future. For example:

- **Long-Term Financial Goal:** Save more money for an emergency fund

    Bite-Sized Goals

    - Establish a monthly budget by the end of January

    - Save $400 per month until December

    - Set up automatic transfer to a savings account by the end of February

    - Cut unnecessary expenses by 10 percent by the end of February

Goal Check: Review and Edit Your Goals

The next phase of intuitive goal setting is knowing how to effectively create your goals. Under the tutelage (I've always wanted to find a way to use that word; it makes me feel super fancy) of my positive psychology coaching mentor, I learned the power of the seven-point goal inspection. Once you create your goal, it's critical to run it through this process to ensure its quality is high enough to maintain its relevance over the next couple of months or through the year.

1. **Self-Efficacy:** This is the belief in your own abilities, specifically your ability to meet the challenges ahead of you and complete a task successfully. *Do I believe I can do this? What would give me the confidence to do this?*

2. **Specificity:** The goal should be specific, measurable, and realistically achievable within a certain length of time. *Can this goal be broken down into smaller chunks? Is this a realistic due date for my current schedule?*

3. **Flow:** You should set goals that stretch you but don't break you. Challenging goals can create growth opportunities, but you want to ensure you're not completely overwhelmed by them. *Is this goal too much or too little?*

4. **Training and Experience:** You should ensure you have the appropriate skills and knowledge to achieve your goals. Many times, when you lack skills or experience in something, it's easier to throw in the towel. *What skills do I need to learn, or what resources/experts do I need to hire?*

5. **Commitment:** Review how dedicated you are to making sure your goal gets accomplished. *How committed am I on a scale of one to ten, with one being not confident and ten being very confident?* If you find you have a low level of commitment, reconsider the goal until you feel more excited about it.

6. **Belief:** You need to decide if this goal really matters to you. *How much of an impact will this have on my intentions for the year? How can I map this from beginning to completion to ensure I'm successful?*

7. **Feedback:** Enlist feedback from peers or colleagues to sharpen your achievement strategy. Create check-in channels via text, email, or over the phone to help hold yourself accountable and remain open to pivot if needed. *Who can I recruit to give me constructive feedback?*

CHAPTER CHALLENGE

Hey, now! It's time to put what we've learned about intuitive goal setting to the test. I consider this way of goal setting more like an experiment than an actual standard, so try it out and see how your old way of setting goals stands up to this new approach. Whatever you decide is the answer to your goal-setting prayers, so don't be stingy. Share it with at least one friend before the week is out. Trust me, they will begin to notice you are out here kicking ass and taking names.

Not only will you be aligned from within because of the work done in the previous chapters, but you might start walking a little differently once those personal and professional wins start piling up. Your friends and family might even ask what you are doing differently, and that's when you can show off your inner Iyanla Vanzant and say, "I decided that I needed to take a more intuitive approach to my life." I can see you now, clear as day. I hope you'll be able to see it too once you try this intuitive goal-setting approach.

The Invitation: Set your timer for thirty minutes and follow the seven-step process for intuitive goal setting.

1. **Visualize Your 365:** If you completed the previous chapter check-in, congrats! You can check this box and move to the next step.

2. **Feel It First:** Using the five areas of well-being, answer the following question: How do I want to feel within the next three months/six months/year?

3. **Set Your Goals and Break Them Down:** Write out your top three long-term goals. Every Sunday review these goals and write down two bite-sized actions you can complete for each one during the week.

4. **Review and Edit:** Run it through the seven-point goal inspection and edit your short-term goals as needed.

5. **Get It Done:** Don't hesitate. Start with one small action at a time. You don't need all the answers. Get creative on how you complete these actions. Remember, done is better than perfect.

6. **Count Your Wins:** At the end of the week, ask yourself the following questions: What went well? What didn't go well? What did I learn?

7. **Pivot and Push Forward:** Decide what you want/need to do differently for your next week of goal setting. Tweak as necessary and run it up again!

BONUS CHALLENGE

Before you head out, I wanted to walk you through what an annual
review process would look like in practice. Personally, I've found that
completing my own annual review each year creates a full picture reflection of my growth and helps me discover any underlying patterns that
exist across the different areas of well-being and how I might set more
realistic and attainable goals for the upcoming year. Similarly, this type
of insight can help you fast-track the achievement of your goals.

The Invitation: Locate your goals and intentions from the prior year.
Find a quiet place where you will not be disturbed, set a timer for thirty
to forty-five minutes, and answer the following questions:

• What goal did I make the least progress on and why?

• What goal am I most proud of achieving?

• What do I want to leave behind?

• What was the biggest lesson I learned?

• What was my favorite memory?

As you progress further on your transformation journey and begin to
achieve the goals you set out for yourself, I hope you continue to use visualization as a guiding light to access your innermost desires and dreams.

With the tools you've gathered from this chapter, I hope that you will continue to set intuitive goals for yourself that inspire but do not overwhelm you. This pursuit of effective goal setting demands more than just ambition; it also calls us to access more internal resources, such as our willpower and self-compassion, to better manage our energy and achieve the intentions we set for ourselves. In the next chapter, we'll dive into how we can harness these powerful skills to effect positive change both within and outside of ourselves.

CHAPTER 10

WHERE THERE IS A WILL, THERE IS A WAY

Using Willpower and Self-Compassion to Unlock Authentic Success

When I go back home to Greenville, South Carolina, there are three nonnegotiable stops I have to make or I will definitely catch that Southern smoke when they see me again: my mom, nieces, and nephews (they are usually at the same stop); Grandma Georgia; and Grandpa Gene.

My Grandma Georgia and Grandpa Gene are my dad's parents who I am surprisingly really close with considering that my dad and I aren't that close. Not to tell their business and all, but they never married so these visits require me to make two different stops.

Every time I visit my grandpa, I can't help but be amazed by his incredible skin. He has this dark reddish-brown tone that remains flawless, even in his mid-eighties. Not to mention, he still manages to, as he says, "go fishing" with the ladies. I always have the same conversations with my grandpa when we get together. Topic one is always about my dad.

Topic two trails into updates about my little sister on my dad's side. Topic three is the latest on my grandmother's health. Then our final destination is his own health and how he has managed to escape the prescription drug hustle that's running rampant in senior citizen homes around the country. I like to get him going so I ask the same question every time I see him, "Now, you look too good and walk around here being too healthy to be in your eighties! What's your secret?"

He loves it so much. "I never smoked or drank a day in my life. I eat good. I get outside in the sunlight and do my landscaping business. I take care of my mind. Talk to myself good, and I don't fool with no nonsense people."

"I know that's right!" I say. I love to pump him up.

His answer is consistent every time, and it never fails to inspire me. Now, his guilty pleasure is going to eat out at the local buffet in town, but even then, he is intentional about his portion sizes.

"I just like that I can get a variety of food in one place," he says.

He likes to explain. He doesn't play about his weight either. His lifestyle choices and commitment to staying active make him a remarkable role model for what life could look like in our eighties.

Thinking about my grandfather often prompts me to consider my own wellness goals. However, let me tell you that white cheddar popcorn and a medium- to full-body red wine are haters to my goals. Here is the problem: whenever I've had a busy week juggling various responsibilities in my business or dealing with ongoing family issues back home, I find myself seeking solace in these indulgences. You know how it goes when the stress is high and rest is low. Those days are the danger zone for my self-discipline. When I'm not on my best behavior, it's easy to turn to snacking and sipping to close out the week.

I realize that I will not be able to keep my PYT status if I continue to let the snacks and sips disrupt my health goals. In honest moments with coaching clients, self-control around health goals tends to be one of the most common conversations. Yes, we laugh at ourselves because you cannot take life too seriously, but then I eventually put on my coaching hat to strategize healthier ways to cope and manage stress while being supportive and gentle during the process.

So much has unfolded with us since chapter one, and I want to share my full appreciation for you hanging in this with me. If you have been working through each chapter challenge and check-in, I know you have had a few uncomfortable moments with yourself. Just know that you are providing a wonderful service to your mind, body, and soul. My hope is that you offer yourself grace and care while showing up to each chapter with a beginner's mind and childlike curiosity.

As you continue doing the hard internal work, there will come a time when a little self-compassion is needed. Goal attainment does not come to fruition exclusively on a wing and a prayer. At some point, you will need some backup. Accessing your willpower through self-regulation and self-compassion is going to carry you through, not only in achieving your goals but also maintaining the changes you've created around your thoughts, behaviors, and habits—especially those that feel a bit harder to break through like, say, your physical and dietary goals.

In this chapter, I want to introduce you to the connection between willpower and self-compassion. You'll learn strategies to manage your will-power to boost your discipline and also how to lean into self-compassion as a way to support yourself through the growth process. Growth doesn't happen in a straight line. Sometimes you zig. Sometimes you zag. And sometimes you take a nap in the middle of the day to reset. Understanding how to manage and utilize your innate internal resources with self-regulation will help you enhance your resiliency for the life shifts you're hoping to create.

Self-regulation is the ability to manage your behavior, which allows you to effectively achieve goals, foster positive outcomes, and prevent negative consequences. People who have higher levels of self-regulation tend to navigate conflict and deal with stress easier than people with limited self-regulation. The development of self-regulation starts in childhood. If you have positive examples from your parents and have access to warm and structured living environments where you feel safe to make mistakes and take risks, your self-regulation will tend to be more developed. One common reason why someone might have limited self-regulation skills is because they never learned how to manage their emotions in a healthy way and still haven't acquired the skills to do so.

In everyday life, limited self-regulation could look like struggling to control your behavior in several areas. For example, you could find it hard to resist eating chocolate or candy when you're hoping to lose weight, or you could fly off the handle with anger one day and suppress your emotions the next. If there was one internal resource that could use a set of jumper cables in my well-being picture, it would be my self-regulation. The way the pandemic came through and disrespected my routines and discipline . . . whew, Lord! I'm still finding pieces of my self-control and healthy habits under the living room couch. But again, growth and well-being is a continuum, and you can be flourishing in January and trying to figure out how to get back to neutral in July. The beauty is in the power of the reset, right? Right.

CHAPTER CHECK-IN

When you don't remember what a certain version of success looks like, you can always find a model of it as inspiration.

The Invitation: Grab your journal and reflect on the following questions:

- When or where is self-regulation hardest for you?
  (Ex: Overeating when you're stressed)

- What beliefs or mind chatter do you have about this
  particular behavior? (Ex: I deserve this extravagant
  meal because . . .)

Oftentimes, you'll see the word *self-regulation* used interchangeably with willpower. Both words relate to a level of control, but psychology researchers have a slight variation in how they define them. While self-regulation is your ability to manage your behavior and emotions, willpower is your ability to resist short-term temptations in order to achieve your long-term goals. Social psychologist Roy Baumeister conducted an experiment using cookies and radishes that suggested that everyone has a limited supply of willpower each day. I can't have you out here not knowing the full story, so boom, this is what happened.[1]

- First, he offered one group freshly baked chocolate chip cookies and told the other group to resist the cookies and snack on radishes instead.

- Then, he gave each group the same impossible puzzle to solve.

- The group who ate the fresh baked cookies worked on the puzzle for nineteen minutes; however, the group who resisted the cookies could only focus on the puzzle for eight minutes.

- His interpretation: Basically, the group who used their willpower to resist temptation told Baumeister (and I'm paraphrasing), "Uh-uh, get somebody else to do it." They simply did not have enough energy to fully engage in an additional willpower challenge.

Essentially, Baumeister and other researchers discovered that will-power is similar to a muscle. When we spend a lot of time on activities that demand discipline, our willpower muscle becomes depleted. Researchers also agree that willpower is connected to success in every area of well-being. And, goodness, it might prove challenging to prioritize all of the well-being areas because you use the same stock of willpower to do any and every kind of task throughout the day. Especially in our fast-paced society, navigating a typical day can often lead to decision fatigue, the concept that your ability to make choices gets weaker as you keep making them.

So, what can you do about this? How do we make sure our will-power stands the test of time instead of depleting? Just like a muscle, Baumeister suggests we train it to make it stronger. You can do this by engaging in easy tasks that help you focus on your self-discipline. For example, for a few weeks, you can practice using your nondominant hand to do small tasks you would typically do with your dominant hand, like opening doors or turning the lights on. The goal here is to work our brain to the point where we are able to resist immediate gratification if it means we're one step closer to our goal. These small discipline tasks may seem unrelated to the bigger goal, but their impact on your willpower muscle cannot be understated. They will also work to alleviate decision fatigue.

Another word I use interchangeably with decision fatigue is *ego depletion*, which is when you use all your available willpower supply for the day. Similar to decision fatigue, if your willpower is used up for the day it will be challenging for you to commit to your personal goals, such as eating a healthier snack versus reaching for a bag of chips. If you are experiencing ego depletion, you may find it increasingly difficult to focus on anything that requires mental energy as your day progresses. As a result, it can impact every area of well-being, including your social interactions.

Let's say you are typically a patient parent with your children, but after a long day of work, you feel completely wiped out. When you walk in the door, it's World War III between your six-year-old and five-year-old. Your depleted self might not react in the gentlest way when trying to calm down the troops, leading to more stress in the home. Your inability to effectively handle your emotions and self-regulate leaks out into every interaction. This is why it's important to figure out how to refuel yourself when your tank is empty.

To combat this, you could focus on *ego repletion* instead, which is the act of intentionally refueling your cognitive resources. Intentional ego repletion is just as important as building your self-awareness, managing your emotions, and creating intuitive goals. There are quite a few ways you can refill your cup. You'll want to incorporate these energizing activities into your daily routine. Some popular ones include:

- **Taking naps and getting your rest:** Being exhausted is the quickest way to keep your pool of resources low. It's important that you get enough sleep every night (six to eight hours for the average adult) and take naps when your body asks for them.

- **Practicing mindfulness and meditation:** Well, look at how things are connecting! Research suggests that daily meditation can support your focus and self-discipline, even after the meditation has been completed.[2]

- **Boost your mood:** Focusing on being in a positive mood can help you refuel when you're feeling depleted. There is research that shows people who watched comedy shows saw an increase in self-control.[3]

CHAPTER CHECK-IN

Now that you've seen some examples of ego repletion activities, it's your turn to brainstorm a custom list of willpower energizers.

The Invitation: Set a three- to five-minute timer and answer the following reflection questions:

- To support my ego repletion, what healthy habits or intentional actions can I use from my self-care toolkit?

- Are there any other activities I can do that I haven't considered yet?

Building your awareness around willpower management is vital for remaining to the right of neutral on the well-being continuum. As you continue to enhance your overall well-being, you'll realize that self-control and self-compassion are vital skills to make you more resilient on this path to total transformation. It can be tough to learn where your weaknesses lie, and you may feel out of control before you gain some semblance of control. In these instances, self-compassion is absolutely necessary to remain level-headed and focused on your goals.

According to Kristin Neff, higher levels of self-compassion have been linked to helping people feel happier, more optimistic, more curious, and more connected to others. Compassion focuses on the desire to alleviate suffering within another person, so when you turn compassion inward, you are alleviating suffering within yourself. Internalizing kindness teaches you to self-soothe without lingering in the negativity. Outside of mindset, self-compassion (a.k.a. being your inner bestie) is seriously my other favorite topic to cover in my keynotes and workshops on authentic happiness because it makes such a huge difference in the sustainability of the transformation journey. Before we go deeper into what self-compassion is, let's talk about what self-compassion is not.

- **Self-compassion is not self-pity.** It actually creates more relatedness between yourself and other people's experiences without leaning into feelings of isolation.

- **Self-compassion is not self-indulgence.** It's not about letting yourself off the hook or doing things that are harmful to your well-being. If you need a pick-me-up, you can show yourself kindness, but the key is to find something that is healthy and healing.

- **Self-compassion is not self-esteem.** Self-compassion isn't dependent on external circumstances, nor is it about your perceived value, narcissism, or feeling better than others to feel good about yourself. Self-compassion is related to emotional resilience and greater clarity of self.

Self-compassion is a hot button topic for me because I coach so many women who are masterful with caring and supporting their spouses, children, friends, sorority sisters, and even colleagues, but they are downright terrible at showing themselves the same level of care. For a long time, I was guilty of this myself. Many of us, especially Black women, have become expert caretakers and cheerleaders for everyone around us, but we tend to forget all about ourselves.

Self-compassion is really about giving ourselves the same level of kindness and care as we would give a close friend or loved one during a hard time.

Outside of setting healthy boundaries, becoming a pro at self-compassion is another way to teach people how to treat you. How you treat yourself sets the tone for how other people are going to treat you in your relationships and friendships. When you are on a growth journey and things aren't happening as fast as you'd like or you backslide into old behaviors, self-compassion will help you create a more realistic and stable perspective of your humanity. Positive side effects of practicing self-compassion include decreased anxiety, depression, rumination, and fear of failure.[4] Adding this technique to your self-care toolkit also helps you recover more quickly from setbacks that are bound to happen every now and then.

So, how does this thing called self-compassion work? Let me break it down for you so it can forever and consistently be broken. (If you get that movie reference, you and I could do Sunday brunch anytime!)

SELF-COMPASSION IS THE ACT OF BEING KIND TO YOURSELF

One way to be kinder to yourself is to be more mindful of your inner and outer self-talk. Building awareness around how you speak to yourself contributes to both your confidence and emotional stability. What does this look like in practice? You can try words of love or positive affirmations, which are statements and phrases that support your core values and counteract harmful or unproductive thoughts. Not only are affirmations useful for your mental health, there is also research out there that suggests that the consistent use of positive affirmations can help combat health-deteriorating stress.[5]

I love using written affirmations within my personal self-care toolkit, as there are recent studies that suggest that writing affirmations helps cultivate positive life decisions, boost self-confidence, and increase motivation. This is extremely helpful for short-term and long-term goal setting.

A few of my favorite self-love phrases are:

- I'm proud of who I am. I'm proud of who I am becoming.

- I trust myself. Every decision I make today will add to, and not subtract from, my life.

- Everything around me is working in my favor. I feel supported, safe, and loved.

If you're new to affirmations or have the desire to write your own, here are a few tips to keep in mind.

SELF-COMPASSION IS GIVING YOURSELF PERMISSION TO BE HUMAN

This is dedicated to the perfectionists out there. Hey, cousin! Before going to therapy, I dove headfirst into the perfectionist mindset with no regret, thinking that perfectionism is solely about striving to be the best. I know some of you wave that perfectionist flag with pride the way I used to, but I just want you to come sit beside me for a second as I say this with love: your worth is not tied to your achievement, perfectionism is not the same thing as excellence, and finally (my favorite saying of all time), done is better than perfect. If you're not sure if any of this applies to you, here are seven signs that might give you some insight:

1. You give yourself a hard time when you make a mistake.

2. You hold yourself to ridiculously higher rules and standards than other people in your life.

3. You procrastinate out of fear of being wrong or making a mistake.

4. You feel guilty about relaxing.

5. You spend more time achieving goals than spending time with the people you love.

6. You have issues with feeling like you're enough.

7. Your motto is "All or nothing."

If you cringed a little reading any of these, then darling, you might have a thing with perfectionism. But listen, that's totally okay. You can't heal what you don't reveal, right? Building your awareness around your dance with perfectionism and calling it out is part of the work. As a recovering perfectionist, there are a few ways I exercise my self-compassion muscles to honor my humanity.

First, I ask myself what support I would give to my best friends at this moment, then I turn that support around on myself. For example, a few months before my birthday I had this big lofty goal of losing twenty pounds, but two weeks before my birthday gathering the scale had other plans. Instead of indulging in a good old-fashioned downward spiral, I reminded myself that regardless of what the scale said a few things were true: my worth isn't measured by what the scale says, thick thighs save lives, and my face card never declines. I put on a cute black dress, threw on some Ruby Woo, and headed for the door!

Next, I remind myself that it's okay to be imperfect because true perfection is not real. And finally, I lean into constructive criticism. This one right here took the longest for me to practice. I still have to remind myself that feedback is data that helps me learn and grow. I'm not always right, and neither are you (yep, I said it!).

SELF-COMPASSION IS BEING MINDFUL OF HOW YOU HANDLE YOUR PERCEIVED WEAKNESSES AND FAILURES

Remember that failure is also data. When I feel myself spiraling, I remind myself that I never fail; I either win or lose. I also ask myself a coaching question I learned during my training: "Will this even matter in a year?" More than likely, the answer is no. If the answer is yes, then I know this is an opportunity to carve out some time and thoughtfully create a game plan to move forward in a different way. In this case, I would collaborate with someone I trust and value so we can co-create ideas and I can feel confident that I'm heading in the right direction.

When we get into the habit of giving ourselves the same kindness and care that we give our closest friends, we create space to heal, grow, break, and put ourselves back together again.

CHAPTER CHALLENGE

As we close out this chapter on willpower and self-compassion, I want to pause for a moment so you can check in on your new best friend: you!

The Invitation: Set your timer for three to five minutes. Take three deep cleansing breaths (inhale through your nose and exhale out your mouth). Grab your journal or, if you're feeling jazzy, a few sticky notes, and complete the following statements. Write the first thing that comes to your mind. Give yourself permission to think, feel, and love on yourself.

- I love myself when . . .
- I'm proud when . . .
- I feel hopeful when . . .
- I am happiest when . . .
- I am inspired when . . .

If you aren't ready for affirmations or they don't feel accessible to you just yet, try writing down two to three ways you can show yourself more kindness versus judgment when you feel like things aren't going so well.

I hope you leave this chapter feeling a little more prepared to not only manage your willpower but also replenish it when you are running low. An important component of greater self-care is to have the capacity to support ourselves the same way we would support our best friend or favorite sibling. Self-compassion allows you to embrace your flaws, honor your needs, and introduce more kindness into your inner dialogue. Treating yourself with more love and compassion paves the way for a transformation journey filled with grace and inner peace. In the next chapter, we'll dig into the role your social connections play in your ability to thrive instead of simply survive.

CHAPTER 11

WHAT ABOUT YOUR FRIENDS?

Leveraging Social Connections for Support and Collective Accountability

The first time I heard about fibroids as a hidden epidemic dispropor-tionately affecting Black women was a few years ago in a group chat. During the pandemic, the group chats with my friends became our new Sunday paper as we connected over funny memes and GIFs, financial and market news, celebrity gossip, and of course the latest health trends. Out of everything we discussed during those challenging times, our conversation on Black women and fibroids stuck with me the most. I didn't know much about them at the time, so I spent time on Google researching symptoms from a few reputable outlets and realized, *Damn. I think I might have fibroids.*

As of the writing of this chapter, I have reached the end of my six-week recovery period from surgery. All in all, I had twenty-five noncancerous tumors (fibroids) removed from my body by way of a laparoscopic myo-mectomy. While I am grateful that my surgery and recovery period were deemed successful, I'm more grateful for the village of people who sup-ported me from the day before my surgery to the last week of recovery.

My best friend from middle school organized a meal train and sent it out to my network of friends to provide two weeks of food during my recovery process. The night before the surgery over twenty people gathered on a phone line to pray for my safety and healing. One of my local friends slept on my couch so she could drive me to Baltimore at five o'clock in the morning for the procedure. My other best friend, who is married with a toddler, drove down the morning of my surgery to watch over me and help me get around that first night post-op. The first week of the surgery was physically one of the toughest times in my life. It was also one of the most affirming moments for me with many of my close connections. Friends showed up at my place every day to drop off home-cooked meals, watch Nollywood shows with me, or volunteer to clean and tidy up.

God has blessed me with some really special people in my life. I'm forever grateful for my village of friends who became sisters, strangers who became mentors, and colleagues who became accountability partners.

Meaningful social connections matter.

MEANINGFUL RELATIONSHIPS AND SUPPORT

It comes as no surprise that, as humans, our brains are hardwired to interact and connect with each other.[1] In fact, a major sign of a flourishing adult is their ability to have meaningful connections and quality platonic relationships.[2] The people you invite into your world will either hinder your growth or increase your momentum, which is why it's vitally important you choose your circle carefully.

A meaningful connection is a reciprocal relationship between two people. This type of relationship offers vulnerability, common interests, shared values, and mutual support. Meaningful connections are not the same as your superficial social media followers nor the neighbors you only see when it's time to check your mailbox nor the one-sided friendship that leaves you feeling drained and unloved. Focusing on quality, deep connections is key. You can be connected to hundreds of people and still experience loneliness because of the quality of those connections.

Social connectedness is the degree to which people have and perceive a desired number, quality, and diversity of relationships that create a sense of belonging and being cared for, valued, and supported.[3] Socially connected people tend to have stable and supportive relationships. Regularly experiencing thoughtful and consistent social exchanges increases your feelings of empathy and compassion toward others, helping to build a stronger sense of community. Socially connected people can sense the support of family, friends, and others in their community. Knowing that you have people you can count on improves your ability to recover from stress, anxiety, and depression. Finally, socially connected people have a stronger sense of belonging, which may inspire them to give back to their communities, helping to further build those connections.[4]

As you can see, nurturing meaningful connections can create a major positive boost in every area of your well-being, and that feeling of security will give you the confidence to share your love and gifts with those around you. In my early thirties, I made the commitment to choose connection over isolation. I realized I was the common denominator in my lack of progress in my personal and professional goals. Not only did I want my friends to commit to holding me accountable, but I wanted to do the same for them. I wanted to hold space for them with love and generosity. The investment you make in intentionally choosing your "Presidential Cabinet" is the greatest pathway to wholeness, prosperity, and longevity. When we fail, it's our close-knit connections who help us hold it all together. Every major accomplishment I've experienced in my adult life can be linked back to my meaningful connections.

COLLECTIVE ACCOUNTABILITY

Every time I've made exponential progress on a personal or professional goal, I can relate it back to the people who were in my corner at that time. Collective accountability focuses on surrounding yourself with individuals who will support you and challenge you as you strive to reach your greatest outcomes. Again, this is a two-way street. Whatever your village of supporters pour into you, you are signing up to provide a similar effort of support, and vice versa. We don't have time for one-sided, draining relationships.

When you invest in holding yourself and your community members accountable, you can ask for specific support based on your individual interests or level of expertise. Creating an ecosystem of people and resources you can count on can help you save time and potentially money on outside resources.

Prior to the pandemic, I spent full weekends with my sister-friends. It was just us, our laptops, a list of weekly goals, and phenomenal vegan tacos. Growing up, I always envisioned having a *Girlfriends* friend group in my life, as one of my favorite pastimes is spending my afternoons cackling about dating in our thirties and joking about our latest weight loss solutions while also loving our bodies at any size. Some of our favorite topics include self-care, the power of manifesting, transparency about our life mistakes, and even affirming each other's dopeness when things seem a bit shaky. I call my diverse group of friends my Presidential Cabinet, inspired by my friend, Tomkins. I even coach my clients in creating their own cabinet.

This small group of women (and a few men) have been my lifeline and informal board of trusted advisors for the past decade. My village consists of friends from childhood, sorority sisters, ex-church members, and even old colleagues from previous work environments. This trusted group of advisors continues to provide love, trust, guidance, and even critical feedback that allow me to pivot in the best ways. They hold me accountable to my goals and inspire me to be my best because they also strive to be the best versions of themselves. So what does this level of support look like for me in real life? I'm glad you asked.

I reach out or connect with my Presidential Cabinet when:

- I need someone to pray over me or with me.

- I need to get some fresh air and go for a walk.

- I'm wondering if my latest idea is genius or lame.

- I need specific accountability for new goals I set for myself. One friend is my health accountability partner. I have two friends who are holding me accountable for my business goals. I have another friend who appointed herself as the keeper of love life talks.

- I'm invited to do a consulting gig, and I'm wondering how much to charge.

- I'm trying to choose the right branding for a new coaching offer and need some input. (I love a good group poll!)

- I'm exhausted from the earth being ghetto and need a funny conversation to take my mind off it.

Researchers believe there are five main dimensions of friendships: closeness, companionship, conflict, help, and security. These five dimensions are critical indicators of friendship's importance from adolescence to emerging adulthood.[5] If I were to take creative license, which I plan to, I would add accountability as the sixth dimension of friendship. Oftentimes, we think about accountability on an individual level, but with my Presidential Cabinet, accountability and support are key elements that are reciprocated across the board. Most of the work we've covered in this book has focused on an intense review and edit of your internal resources, but it's important you also spend some time reviewing your social resources. So, let's jump right in and practice now!

CHAPTER CHALLENGE

For this chapter challenge, I invite you to examine your Presidential Cabinet. We know that change and growth are largely inside jobs, but accountability and support make up the glue that keeps you on track. Consider who will hold you accountable to the reconstruction of your belief systems, new mindsets, and self-compassion practices. Who will remind you of your value when you forget? Who will hold space for you to be ratchet and righteous within the same conversation? It's time to be more intentional about your village.

Before I set you out into the wild to build your Presidential Cabinet, there are a few guidelines I typically share with my coaching clients that I'd love to share with you as well. Your Presidential Cabinet should include people who:

- Energize you and support a life of ease and efficiency

- Consider you for opportunities when you're not in the room

- Encourage you to prioritize your mental and emotional well-being

- Show mutual support and respect

The Invitation: Set a timer for fifteen to twenty minutes, and in your journal, respond to the following questions:

- Who's in your Presidential Cabinet, and how do they support you?

- Who do you need to add, and how will they support your journey?

- If you change nothing, what will your life look like three months from now? How does this make you feel?

BONUS CHALLENGE

Think of one connection you'd like to be more intentional about exploring. Invite this person out for a coffee date, or if it's nice outside, ask if they'd be interested in a walk and talk. Remember, your meaningful connections are just as valuable as everything else in your self-care toolkit, so choose wisely!

Your social connections are the anchor that nourishes growth and fuels your ability to truly thrive. Being a keeper of meaningful relationships brings so much richness, significance, and sense of belonging to your life. As we shift into the next chapter, I invite you to grab your curiosity and refresh your favorite beverage; this one's going to be good!

CHAPTER 12

HUSTLE AND FLOW

Creating an Engaged Life

Are you Caribbean?" Mandy's friend Tonya asked me.

"No, but I love Caribbean music and can have a good time anywhere," I replied.

"Oh, okay—but are you comfortable with partner dancing with
strangers?" she said with a little bit of concern tied to her voice.

"Girl, I will be fine. You're Haitian, right? So is this a Koompa party?"
I asked, feeling proud of myself because, yes, your girl is cultured.

"Yes! It's a *Konpa* dance party," she gently corrected me.

"Okay then, I'll get the tickets and meet y'all at the first spot."

It was the Founders Day celebration for my sorority, and we were
headed to happy hour in downtown DC. My friend Mandy invited me
to partake in the post-celebration shenanigans with her and a friend, and
called her friend on speaker phone so she could explain the vibes for the
rest of the evening. After a round of libations, ad hoc party-walking, and
a unified singing of the Black negro spiritual "Knuck If You Buck," we
closed out our checks at the bar and headed to Silver Spring, Maryland,
for the party.

If I'm being honest, I'd been obsessed with Konpa videos for the past year. I was intrigued by the closeness and intimacy of the dance. So having an opportunity to see it up close and personal was right up my alley. Because we were fashionably late, we missed the instructional section of the night and people were already partnered up on the dance floor swaying to the music. Tonya looked at both Mandy and me and said, "Either of you want a quick tutorial before we go out into the wild?" I quickly raised my hand and she gave me a two-minute demo of the basic moves.

"I think I can do this," I said. I had a little confidence in my ability to catch on, as I used to teach Zumba classes part-time at LA Fitness a few years back. I also knew a little merengue, bachata, and salsa. How hard could this be?

"Okay, don't worry if you've never done this before. If you find a dance partner, they are really cool about leading you. If you have a little bit of rhythm and know how to follow, you should be fine," Tonya said and then she disappeared into the wild.

"Okay. Open mind, open heart," I quietly said to myself as I watched the crowd sway and two-step to the beautiful sounds of drums and horns. Just as I was about to take a seat, a guy walked up swaying to the music and extended his hand, inviting me to the dance floor.

"Ehhh. I don't really know how to do this," I said. He just smiled, shrugged his shoulders, and pulled me out to the dance floor. I kept trying to explain that, one, I wasn't Haitian, and two, I didn't know this dance. With his thick accent, he gently pulled me closer and said, "Follow me. Just dance." So I did.

After about ten to fifteen minutes of awkwardly stepping over my feet and onto his, I found my sweet spot. My dance partner barely spoke English but still tried to make small talk as we danced.

"Parlez-vous français?" he said, trying to find a common language.

"Uhhhh. Je parle un petit peu français," I managed to pull from what I remembered from high school French class, but it still wasn't enough for a coherent conversation. We both settled on just feeling the vibes, and I finally started to relax and lean into trusting my dance partner.

Without words, he gently guided me to the right direction if I went the wrong way, smiling and leading me with care. It felt safe and intentional. Once he realized I had the hang of it, he started teaching me little arm tricks, a few subtle turns and babayyy, I was into it! It felt like time slowed down. Even though the room was full of people, it felt like the two of us were in our own little world, stepping and swaying to the music in perfect harmony. It was the first time in a long time that I felt deeply immersed in an experience—my whole mind and body.

At some point in the night, I broke out of my trance and looked at my watch. *Oh wow, it's late!* I'd literally been dancing for hours and didn't even notice. I looked over at Tonya and Mandy, who were standing to the side with that ready to go look. *Damn.* I looked at my dance partner and tried to remember how to say goodnight.

Somehow I mustered up, "Uhhh . . . Partir, au revoir!" Again, my French was terrible, but the brother understood what I was trying to say. He smiled and then gave me a big hug.

"Bonne nuit," he said.

The three of us walked outside and headed toward our cars. The endorphins were still having a party in my body, and then I looked over at my reflection in the venue window. *Dammit, I sweat out my silk press!*

My experience of losing track of time and feeling completely immersed in my dancing is what positive psychologist Mihaly Csikszentmihalyi describes as a state of flow.[1] Flow is a positive state of being when you are deeply focused and involved in something that usually you're also very skilled at doing. When you experience flow, you are completely immersed in the activity, with your entire mind and body engaged. Nothing else around you matters during that time period as you are completely and totally minding your business while feeling in the zone. Because we are all individuals, there are different ways we can get to and experience flow.

When I think about real-life examples of someone in a flow state, my mind immediately goes to jazz musicians. They might have scheduled a simple one-hour practice, but before long, the practice turns into an impromptu three-hour jam session with songs that weren't even on the set list, thanks to Frank the saxophone player. When I think about flow state,

I think of basketball players like Steph Curry, who are able to get in the zone and effortlessly drop three pointers all game long. Basically, a flow experience can occur when you're focused on an activity you deeply enjoy and are more than likely really dope at. Let me tell you what isn't considered a flow state: binge watching Netflix or scrolling through the 'gram. A flow state involves being in a deep state of concentration and being fully absorbed in something that provides you a sense of achievement. The key to achieving a flow state is accessing it through productive and creative tasks that yield the greatest return for our mind, body, and spirit.

WHY FLOW MATTERS

Let me tell you something: there will never be a time when pain, sorrow, or disappointment are going to cease to exist in our lives. The tools we've been experimenting with throughout the book will not only help you grow and shift into the person you've always wanted to be, but you can also experience joy along the way.

The question is, how do we extend those joyful and meaningful moments? Let's take it one step further. Instead of moments, how do we lean into longer optimal experiences? You know, those experiences that help you feel good, think good, and do good. You guessed it, boo! You have to go with the flow.

Despite not being able to prevent disasters, family deaths, and other hardships that are a natural part of life, tapping into flow helps you feel more in control of your life and happiness. So instead of being frustrated by how hard life can get or how bored you are in your day-to-day routine, you have the power to focus on doing things you love to do. Creating this optimal experience (a.k.a. flow state) helps you remain present and not worry about tomorrow or ruminate on what happened last night. If you're into curating a more meaningful and joyful existence, then you need to ask yourself at this moment: *How can I actively enjoy my life to its greatest potential while pursuing the things I love?* The answer is to learn how to tap into flow.

First, let me give you my very basic view of how this works. The two things you need to consider when looking to achieve flow are your goals and self-reflection—you want to have a goal or something you need to complete. As you're working to complete the goal, you want to reflect on the experience of it. This self-reflection gives you information about how it's working for you. So remember, flow happens when you are completely in the zone, right? The way you get into the zone is by finding something you really enjoy doing. The key is to strike a balance between this activity being challenging but also something you have the skill to do. You don't want it to be too challenging (that will frustrate you or make you anxious) or too easy (you'll just get bored). For example, let's say you enjoy running after work on Tuesdays and Thursdays. When you started this routine three months ago, it was challenging but also rewarding because the mini hills in your neighborhood kept you on your toes. Now when you lace up your shoes for a run, you don't feel as motivated for the jog. This would be a perfect time for you to switch things up. To make it challenging again, you could find steeper hills to add to your route or maybe search for new routes altogether. You could even keep a list of routes for whenever you feel things getting stale.

When you find the balance between challenge and skill, this is where you will experience feeling in the zone or in a flow state. Although, being in flow may look different for you than it does for me, there are eight universal characteristics of any flow state experience.

1. **Clear Goals.** Of course, the first thing you want to do is decide on a specific and clear goal for your task. If you are a runner, you must decide if you want to run three miles or if you want to run for thirty minutes.

2. **Concentration.** You also want to make sure you have complete concentration on the task or activity. This means removing anything that might be a distraction. I will go as far as putting my cell phone in another room or even removing my social media apps for the time period if that's what it will take to help me get into my zone.

3. **Balance Between Difficulty and Skill Level.** As I pointed out earlier, your activity aligns with your skill level, but you always want to make sure you find a healthy balance between challenging but not overwhelming. Finding this perfect in-between place is what will help you get into the zone.

4. **Transformation of Time.** I mentioned this a bit earlier, but when you're experiencing flow while working on something, you may lose track of time. Hours can go by and you won't even notice it.

5. **Intrinsically Rewarding.** The fifth characteristic of a flow state is that the experience has to be rewarding and bring you pleasure. You should feel a sense of accomplishment and happiness when you're done with your activity.

6. **Feels Effortless.** Flow also involves having a sense of effortlessness. While you're in the midst of your activity or task, you should be able to navigate it with relative flexibility. You often see this with athletes where they can pivot on the fly and still make plays happen without taking too much time to think or ruminate.

7. **Action and Awareness Merge.** Not only is there a loss of time when you're in a flow state, but your actions and awareness will put you into autopilot. You're fully aware of your activity, but you feel tapped into what you're working on and you're completing it intuitively and with ease.

8. **Sense of Control.** Finally, when you're having a flow experience, you feel a sense of control and confidence. With your knowledge and skill level, you have control over the result of your activity and this helps to keep you in a flow state as well.

To me, flow feels like a best-kept secret in how to make the most out of our human experience. One of my many intentions in this life is to not focus so much on the future that it gives me anxiety and not to dwell too much on the past that it pushes me toward depression. What would life be like if you created more flow in your day-to-day life? This can apply to work or recreation. Flow is like a cheat code to being more productive and creative. Not only will you be able to stretch yourself while operating in your zone of genius, but this state trains you to be more open and in touch with who you are, what you love, and how you can do things better.

This is a come-to-Jesus moment for you. I am inviting you to explore how you can bring more flow experiences into your life. Sure, this will help you find your sweet spot, but a byproduct of this optimal experience is that you can continue to build a life filled with joy, pleasure, and meaning. You can't beat that with a stick!

CHAPTER CHECK-IN

Now that you know what flow is and what it looks like when you're in a flow state, let's explore what flow means for your own life.

The Invitation: Grab something to capture your thoughts and find a quiet place to reflect. Close your eyes and take a deep breath. Now, think about the last time you were completely in the zone, a time where you were immersed in something and felt pure bliss and achievement. This can be a recent or distant memory, just as long as it's vivid enough for you to capture it in a few sentences.

Write a brief description about this experience, highlight what you did, where you were, how you felt, and if you can recall how long this experience lasted. If you need some inspiration, revisit my Konpa dance story.

If you're having a hard time recalling a specific flow moment, don't worry; instead, you can write down a list of activities you absolutely love to do. Don't hold back here. Write down any hobbies, recreational sports, or passion projects that bring you a deep sense of enjoyment and energy. Don't forget to include things that have a diverse range in difficulty and skill level that helps keep things exciting. Beside each item on this list, write down its challenge level from low to high. For example:

- Tending to my indoor plant family (low challenge)
- Exploring new recipes for dinner (moderate challenge)

- Writing short stories about millennial Black women
  (high challenge)

- Indoor rock climbing to conquer new levels and climbs
  (high challenge)

I hope this check-in gives you the courage to keep exploring what truly lights you up and to move through life with a spirit of curiosity. Carry these insights with you as you create more ripples of fulfillment and inspiration for the journey. Go on and flow on, sis!

A SIDEBAR ABOUT VITALITY

I couldn't leave this chapter without talking about the importance that vitality plays on this transformation journey, and it just so happens that it is a byproduct of tapping into a flow state. Black people, especially Black women, spend so much time thinking about safety and how to successfully navigate and dismantle racism and the patriarchy. Although these are extremely important to navigate for survival, I think we should equally continue to find strategies for thriving. Even when I say the word *thrive* out loud, I immediately feel hopeful and encouraged.

Vitality is another bridge we need to cross in order to fully thrive. It refers to a feeling of aliveness and positive energy in your physical and mental well-being. Physically you are feeling healthy and your energy levels are high. You're ready to take on the world. Psychologically, you have a zest for life that inspires you to live out your days with more meaning and purpose. Vitality is an essential strength that plays a central role in your own happiness and well-being. Along with curiosity, hope, gratitude, and love, it is one of the key ingredients that strongly influences overall life satisfaction and a sense of well-being.[2]

I bet when you look up the definition of vitality, you'll find a picture of my Grandpa Gene cheesing with his one finger pointed to the sky (that's his favorite pose). At eighty-four years old, he has mastered his personal formula for maintaining a zest for life. I've never met someone his age who still approaches life with so much vigor.

I know personally I don't want to have to jump out any more perfectly fine planes to experience this type of energy, so to prevent myself from having to do that, my intention is to shift my focus on incorporating vitality as part of my formula for flourishing.

Research shows that having positive social interactions and diverse social conversations throughout the day can significantly boost your vitality. Let me point out again, the key word is POSITIVE interactions. You can't be out here hanging tight with energy vampires; that defeats the whole purpose of what we're trying to do here. Socialize wisely! Unhealthy habits such as smoking, eating poorly, living a sedentary lifestyle, and staying in stressful environments can be detrimental to your vitality. Remember vitality is not just about your physical well-being but also your mental well-being. Those types of habits also can negatively impact your mood and mental health.

But here is what's really dope: people who are dealing with health issues also have the power to access vitality. In studies involving older women and individuals with chronic pain, researchers found that vitality was not solely determined by the severity of physical conditions.[3] Factors like fear of pain and seeking treatment for the wrong reasons can actually mess with your vitality. It's not just about the body; it's about our mindset and the connections we foster.

When it comes to boosting your vitality, there are a few things we can do that really make a difference. First off, prioritize nurturing your social connections. It's in your best interest to make an effort to connect with your friends, spend quality time with loved ones, and participate in activities that bring you closer together. You see how important people are in our well-being journey? One thing remains true: Other People Matter.

But it's not just about the people we surround ourselves with; it's also about taking care of ourselves. Why? Because again, self-care matters! You should continue to be intentional about the food that fuels your body and gives it the energy you need. Remember to also move your body, even if it's just a walk around your neighborhood. It can do wonders for your vitality.

Flow and vitality are the perfect fusion to unlock a life that is centered on happiness, joy, and, most importantly, flourishing. As we approach the final chapter of this incredible journey we've had together, let us light the torch of vitality within us as we step into the next exciting phase of our lives. With renewed energy and a profound appreciation for the beautiful interplay between our body, mind, and the cherished relationships that bring us joy, we can embark on this concluding chapter together, ready to make the most of our most valued treasure: life itself.

CHAPTER 13

GO LIVE YA LIFE

Agreements for Holistic Well-Being

Come on in here, Kee-yonni," my Grandma Georgia said, neglecting the T near the end of my name. As far as she is concerned, it was never there.

"Hey, girl! I see you're still kickin'," I said.

"Yup, I sure am. Still kickin'!"

I sat down in the chair next to my grandmother's hospital bed, staring out of the window before looking over at her. She had been in the same bed, in the same room, for five months now, waiting to get placed in a long-term care facility. It was strange seeing my grandmother that way. She had always been independent, driving herself everywhere, even if it was at twenty-five miles an hour. The hospital life was new for her as well. Not being able to move around. Not having the ability to go to her kitchen and whip up a meal from scratch. She tried her best to crack a smile for me.

I was in town visiting from "up north," as she would call Washington, DC. I told her I lived in a suburb of DC now, but it was all the same to her. A sepia-colored cowboy show played on the television that she was barely watching, but I couldn't take my eyes off her. She looked so different. So fragile. I turned my attention to the communication board posted at the front of her room that listed the date, the nurse on call, the tech, and her physician. Under "Goals for Your Stay," I read the words "Comfort Care." I don't spend much time in hospitals, so I didn't know what it meant. I pulled out my phone to look it up. "Comfort Care, also known as palliative care, focuses on symptom and pain management for someone who is approaching the end of life." End of life? My heart sank in my chest. I knew my grandmother's cancer had come back. I also knew she decided not to do chemotherapy this time around, but seeing those words while sitting in the hospital made it all feel very real.

Suddenly, my curiosity kicked in and started tapping my spirit. I tried to brush it away, but it kept getting more annoying to push down. I cleared my throat, drank a sip of water, then asked, "Grandma, if you could go back and tell your thirty- or forty-year-old self something you didn't know then, what would you say?"

She turned her head and looked at me thoughtfully. "Well, I-I, let me think about it." She licked her lips and tried to sit up a little bit so she could really see me. "I guess I would tell myself to make sure you take better care of your health. Make sure you pay more attention to ya body and ya mind. I would tell myself to just enjoy ya life. Have more fun. Stop worryin' about everythang. Live ya life how ya want to as long as ya healthy."

My grandma didn't realize that she'd just given me a whole sermon in a few simple words. I thought about her advice during my entire eight-hour drive home. *Prioritize your health. Pay more attention to your mind and body. Make time for play. Don't sweat the small stuff. Live life to the fullest.* Now that's some good stuff, Georgia Mae. Good indeed.

After recovering from "going under the blade" (that's what my friend Coop called my fibroid surgery), those pearls of wisdom from my grandma made their way back into my mind. *Prioritize my health.* During my post-operation appointment, my doctor informed me that bodies that make fibroids will continue to make fibroids. But see, the thing was, I was not trying to go back *under the blade* anytime soon, so I knew I needed to create a game plan and quickly. According to my doctor, there is no proven method to prevent them; however, I can reduce the risk of developing them with a healthier diet and a more active lifestyle. It was time for a mid-year goal shake-up. The goals that mattered most before had to be deprioritized a bit so I could "pay more attention to my body and my mind."

My new weekly diet consists of foods that help heal and prevent inflammation. Because I'm an integrative medicine kind of girl, I've also invested in herbal supplements that support the healing of my reproductive health. Lastly, I have recommitted to three to four days of movement. I felt so energized by my progress that I had to bring in reinforcements for sustainability, so I reinstated my membership at an all-women's gym, hired a chef to make my weekly meals for lunch and dinner, and enlisted my best friend as my accountability partner to do weekly weigh-ins. With these small adjustments, I'm feeling clearer and more confident that I can continue to take care of my body so my body can take care of me in return. Now, I'm not going to lie, change is hard. Yes, even good change, and we've done plenty of that throughout this book. I told you in the beginning and I'm telling you now: I'm in this with you. As we become more aware of our shortcomings, it's up to us to make the change to be better than we were yesterday. As Maya Angelou once said, "When you know better, you do better."[1]

Well, this is my stop here. I believe this is a great place to get off. Before I let you go, I want you to know you should be proud of yourself for getting to the end of this book. We live in a distracted world, and the fact that you were able to finish this book is a major victory. We did a lot of unpacking, unlearning, listening, and reflecting, and hopefully you got a few good chuckles along the way. Throughout our remarkable journey together, we dove into the depths of your self-awareness and well-being, boldly dismantled old mindsets and beliefs, and learned how to intuitively set heart-felt goals. Take a moment to reflect on all the progress you've made and acknowledge and celebrate your accomplishments. You've done so much good work here. You should be so proud of yourself.

THE FINAL CHECK-IN

As you flip through the final pages of this chapter, think about the incredible discoveries you've encountered about your deepest thoughts and desires.

The Final Invitation: Grab a cup of your favorite tea and your journal. I want you to take your time on this final invitation. Before you proceed, take three deep cleansing breaths. Remember to slowly inhale through your nose and exhale through your mouth. After you've done that, respond to the following prompts:

- What are you grateful for?

- What are you most proud of at this moment?

- What have you learned about yourself while completing the check-ins throughout the book?

- What mental shifts have you experienced? What habit changes have you made?

- What are two to three practices you wish to spend more time exploring?

- Who will you share this book with?

Thank you for allowing me to be part of your growth journey. One more thing before you go! Now is the time to wholeheartedly affirm the transformative changes you've made as a result of this book. Let's seal this beautiful bond we share and carry it with us with one last invitation. The following seven personal agreements were designed with you in mind, and by signing this agreement for holistic well-being, you are committing to continuing this transformative journey toward expanding your self-awareness, nurturing a growth mindset, establishing healthy boundaries, and setting intuitive goals.

THE SEVEN AGREEMENTS

- I give myself permission to be human.
- I check in with my thoughts and emotions daily.
- I commit to activities that bring me joy.
- I cultivate healthy communication and connections.
- I make money decisions that support financial liberation.
- I make physical wellness a priority.
- I set and attain goals that honor my soul.

When you agree to uphold these agreements, please place both palms over your heart, inhale through your nose, exhale through your mouth, and say, "I will." Feel free to copy these agreements into your journal and sign it, so you know it's real!

My final hope for you is that you remember that transformation is a journey, not a destination. You have permission to revisit this book at any moment for any number of reasons. Thank you for your time and most importantly, thank you for showing up for yourself chapter by chapter. Finally, I leave you with this: *The light in me honors and cherishes the light in you.* And like Grandma Georgia said, "Remember to live ya life how you want to as long as ya healthy!"

Peace & Blessings,

C

ACKNOWLEDGMENTS

I would like to take a moment to express my deepest gratitude to the many people who have supported and encouraged me throughout the years. Without your love and support, this book would not have been possible. To my beautiful family: my mother; my only living grandmother, Georgia Mae; the only grandfather I've known, Grandpa Gene; and my siblings, nephews, and nieces—your support and encouragement have kept me going, and I am grateful for each and every one of you.

I want to thank my godparents and mentors, the Hiltons, who God sent to me in college to cover me with prayer and their presence. You are two of the wisest, kindest, spiritually grounded, and thoughtful human beings I know. Thank you again for buying me my first car. Thank you for your unwavering support and belief in me.

I am grateful for the support and guidance of several individuals who have been instrumental in my growth and development in the space of positive psychology and personal development coaching: Valerie Burton, Emiliya Zhivotovskaya, and Katie Conlon, your insights and expertise have been invaluable, and I am honored to have had the opportunity to learn from you.

I would also like to acknowledge my Presidential Cabinet. Too many to name here, but you know who you are! I am forever thankful for the space you hold in my personal and business life. Thank you for being my family and loving me unconditionally, spending time, sharing resources, praying for me, and just being present when I needed it most. All of you have poured into me collectively and individually, and I can never thank you enough.

To my phenomenal agent, Felice Laverne, your support and belief in me have been much needed and greatly appreciated. You are a rock star in the industry, and I am honored to have worked with you.

I want to thank my amazing coaching clients for trusting me with your dreams. It has been an honor to serve all of you.

To every speaking and training client who has allowed me to serve your teams and workforces, I appreciate you so much.

Last and certainly not least, I would like to thank you, the reader. I am overwhelmed with a sense of gratitude for your decision to pick up this book. It is an honor to have you as a part of this community of seekers and learners. Please keep me updated on your journey.

NOTES

1 "Janelle Monáe," interview by Angie Martinez, *IRL* podcast, May 17, 2023, video, 4:43 and 53:20, youtube.com/watch?v=agIZkP7Yvnw.

Introduction

1 "Positive psychology definition," Positive Psychology Center, University of Pennsylvania, ppc.sas.upenn.edu/#:~:text=Positive%20Psychology %20is%20the%20scientific,love%2C%20work%2C%20and%20play.

Chapter 1: Self-Aware AF

1 Tasha Eurich, "What Self-Awareness Really Is (and How to Cultivate It)," *Harvard Business Review*, January 4, 2018, hbr.org/2018/01/what-self -awareness-really-is-and-how-to-cultivate-it.

2 "Character Strengths Survey," VIA Institute on Character, viacharacter.org.

3 "Strengths Assessment," Clifton Strengths, Gallup, gallup.com /cliftonstrengths/en/home.aspx.

Chapter 2: In Those Genes

1 Kathy Caprino, "The Top 8 Things People Desperately Desire but Can't Seem to Attain," *Forbes*, May 24, 2016, forbes.com/sites/kathycaprino /2016/05/24/the-top-8-things-people-desperately-desire-but-cant-seem-to -attain/?sh=6739b7907086.

2 Sonja Lyubomirsky, *The How of Happiness: A Scientific Approach to Getting the Life You Want* (New York: Penguin, 2007).

3 Martin E.P. Seligman, *Authentic Happiness: Using the New Positive Psychology to Realize Your Potential for Lasting Fulfillment* (New York: Free Press, 2002).

4   Sonja Lyubomirsky, Kennon M. Sheldon, and David Schkade, "Pursuing Happiness: The Architecture of Sustainable Change," *Review of General Psychology* 9, no. 2 (2005): 111–31, doi.org/10.1037/1089-2680.9.2.111.

Chapter 4: Mind over Mind Chatter

1   Lyn Y. Abramson, Martin E.P. Seligman, and John D. Teasdale, "Learned Helplessness in Humans: Critique and Reformulation," *Journal of Abnormal Psychology* 87, no. 1 (1978): 49–74, doi.org/10.1037 /0021-843X.87.1.49.

2   Gregory M. Buchanan and Martin E.P. Seligman, eds., *Explanatory Style* (New York: Routledge, 1995).

3   Martin E.P. Seligman, *Learned Optimism: How to Change Your Mind and Your Life* (New York: Vintage Books, 2006).

4   Albert Ellis, "The Revised ABC's of Rational-Emotive Therapy (RET)," *Journal of Rational-Emotive & Cognitive-Behavior Therapy* 9, no. 3 (1991): 139–172, doi.org/10.1007/BF01061227.

5   Richard J. Davidson et al., "Alterations in Brain and Immune Function Produced by Mindfulness Meditation," *Psychosomatic Medicine* 65, no. 4 (2003): 564–70, doi.org/10.1097/01.PSY.0000077505.67574.E3.

6   Britta Hölzel et al., "Mindfulness Practice Leads to Increases in Regional Brain Gray Matter Density," *Psychiatry Research* 191, no. 1 (2010): 36–43, doi.org/10.1016/j.pscychresns.2010.08.006.

Chapter 5: Draw the Line

1   Sybil Ottenstein, "3 Biggest Myths about Boundaries: And Why We Need Them," *The Now* (blog), *Psychology Today*, December 10, 2020, psychologytoday.com/us/blog/the-now/202012/3-biggest-myths-about -boundaries.

Chapter 6: Take Care

1   Nicole Martínez et al., "Self-Care: A Concept Analysis," *International Journal of Nursing Sciences* 8, no. 4 (October 2021): 418–25, doi.org/10 .1016/j.ijnss.2021.08.007.

2   Sonja Lyubomirsky, *The How of Happiness: A Scientific Approach to Getting the Life You Want* (New York: Penguin, 2007).

3   Justyna Mróz, "Forgiveness and Flourishing: The Mediating and Moderating Role of Self-Compassion," *International Journal of Environmental Research and Public Health* 20, no. 1 (December 30, 2022): 666, pubmed.ncbi.nlm.nih.gov/36612983/.

4   "John Travis (Physician)/Illness-Wellness Continuum," Wikipedia, Wikimedia Foundation, last modified June 21, 2022, en.wikipedia.org /wiki/John_Travis_(physician).

5   Reshawna Chapple, "Do I Need Therapy?" *TalkSpace* (blog), October 7, 2021, talkspace.com/blog/do-i-need-therapy/.

Chapter 8: Breaking Bad

1   James Clear, *Atomic Habits: An Easy & Proven Way to Build Good Habits & Break Bad Ones* (New York: Avery Publishing, 2018).

Chapter 9: Dreams Unlocked

1   Moshe Bar, ed, *Predictions in the Brain: Using Our Past to Generate a Future* (Oxford: Oxford Academic Books, 2011), doi.org/10.1093/acprof :oso/9780195395518.001.0001.

Chapter 10: Where There Is a Will, There Is a Way

1   Roy F. Baumeister and John Tierney, *Willpower: Rediscovering the Greatest Human Strength* (New York: Penguin Books, 2012).

2   Malte Friese, Claude Messner, and Yves Schaffner, "Mindfulness Meditation Counteracts Self-Control Depletion," *Consciousness and Cognition* 21, no. 2 (2012): 1016–22, doi.org/10.1016/j.concog.2012.01.008.

3   Dianne M. Tice et al., "Restoring the Self: Positive Affect Helps Improve
     Self-Regulation Following Ego Depletion," *Journal of Experimental Social
     Psychology* 43, no. 3 (2007): 379–84, doi.org/10.1016/j.jesp.2006.05.007.

4   Kristin D. Neff, "The Role of Self-Compassion in Development: A
     Healthier Way to Relate to Oneself," *Human Development* 52, no. 4
     (2009): 211–14, doi.org/10.1159/000215071.

5   David K. Sherman et al., "Psychological Vulnerability and Stress: The
     Effects of Self-Affirmation on Sympathetic Nervous System Responses to
     Naturalistic Stressors," *Health Psychology* 28, no. 5 (2009): 554–62, doi.org
     /10.1037/a0014663.

Chapter 11: What About Your Friends?

1   Rivka Rochkind, "Hardwired for Connection," PsychCare, April 14, 2016,
     psychcaremd.com/hardwired-for-connection/#:~:text=Humans%20are
     %20hardwired%20for%20connection,re%20interacting%20with%20other
     %20people.

2   Laura M. Padilla-Walker, Madison K. Memmott-Elison, and Larry J.
     Nelson, "Positive Relationships as an Indicator of Flourishing During
     Emerging Adulthood," in *Flourishing in Emerging Adulthood: Positive
     Development During the Third Decade of Life,* eds. Laura M. Padilla-Walker
     and Larry J. Nelson (New York: Oxford University Press, 2017), 212–36.

3   "Social Connectedness: NCCDPHP's Program Successes," Centers for
     Disease Control and Prevention, National Center for Chronic Disease
     Prevention and Health Promotion, April 18, 2023, cdc.gov/emotional
     -wellbeing/social-connectedness/index.htm.

4   Julianne Holt-Lundstad, Timothy B. Smith, and J. Bradley Leyton,
     "Social Relationships and Mortality Risk: A Meta-Analytic Review," *PLOS
     Medicine* 7, no. 7 (2010), doi.org/10.1371/journal.pmed.1000316; Oscar
     G. Anderson and Colette Thayer, "Loneliness and Social Connections: A
     National Survey of Adults 45 and Older," *AARP Research*, September 2018,
     doi.org/10.26419/res.00246.001; Richard M. Lee, Matthew Draper, and

Sujin Lee, "Social Connectedness, Dysfunctional Interpersonal Behaviors, and Psychological Distress: Testing a Mediator Model," *Journal of Counseling Psychology* 48, no. 3 (2001): 310–18, doi.org/10.1037/0022-0167.48.3.310.

5   Lucia Ponti et al., "A Measure for the Study of Friendship and Romantic Relationship Quality from Adolescence to Early-Adulthood," *The Open Psychology Journal* 3 (2010): 76–87, doi.org/10.2174/1874350101003010076.

Chapter 12: Hustle and Flow

1   Mihaly Csikszentmihalyi, *Flow: The Psychology of Optimal Experience* (New York: Harper Perennial, 2008).

2   Brenda W. Penninx et al., "Emotional Vitality among Disabled Older Women: The Women's Health and Aging Study," *Journal of the American Geriatrics Society* 46, no. 7 (1998): 807–15, doi.org/10.1111/j.1532-5415.1998.tb02712.x.

3   Penninx et al., "Emotional Vitality among Disabled Older Women."

Chapter 13: Go Live Ya Life

1   "The Powerful Lesson Maya Angelou Taught Oprah," Oprah's Life Class, October 19, 2011, oprah.com/oprahs-lifeclass/the-powerful-lesson-maya-angelou-taught-oprah-video.

BIBLIOGRAPHY

Achor, Sean. *The Happiness Advantage*. New York: Random House, 2010

Ackerman, Courtney E. "What Is Self-Awareness? (+ 5 Ways to Be More Self-Aware)." Positive Psychology. April 1, 2020. positivepsychology.com/self-awareness-matters-how-you-can-be-more-self-aware/.

Akhtar, Miriam. "What is Self-Efficacy? Bandura's 4 Sources of Efficacy Beliefs." Positive Psychology. November 8, 2008. positivepsychology.org.uk/self-efficacy-definition-bandura-meaning/.

American Family Care. "Debunking the Myths of Self-Care." Blog. April 20, 2020. afcurgentcare.com/blog/debunking-the-myths-of-self-care/.

American Psychological Association. "What You Need to Know about Willpower: The Psychological Science of Self-Control." American Psychological Association. 2012. apa.org/helpcenter/willpower.

Baumeister, Roy F., Ellen Bratslavsky, Mark Muraven, and Dianne M. Tice. "Ego Depletion: Is the Active Self a Limited Resource?" *Journal of Personality and Social Psychology* 74, no. 5 (1998): 1252–65. doi.org/10.1037//0022-3514.74.5.1252.

Baumeister, Roy F., and John Tierney. *Willpower: Rediscovering the Greatest Human Strength*. New York: Penguin Books, 2012.

Buck, Chad A. "Establishing Effective Personal Boundaries." Vanderbilt Faculty and Staff Health and Wellness. vumc.org/health-wellness/resource-articles/establishing-effective-personal-boundaries.

Carson, James W., Kimberly M. Carson, Karen M. Gil, and Donald H. Baucom. "Mindfulness-Based Relationship Enhancement." *Behavior Therapy* 35, no. 3 (Summer 2004): 471–94. doi.org/10.1016/S0005-7894(04)80028-5.

Centers for Disease Control and Prevention. "Social Connectedness."
National Center for Chronic Disease Prevention and Health Promotion,
Division of Population Health. Last reviewed March 31, 2023. cdc.gov
/emotional-wellbeing/social-connectedness/index.htm.

Chappell, Reshawna. "Do I Need Therapy?" Blog. *TalkSpace*, October 7,
2021. talkspace.com/blog/do-i-need-therapy.

Condon, Paul, Gaëlle Desbordes, Willa B. Miller, and David DeSteno.
"Meditation Increases Compassionate Responses to Suffering."
Psychological Science 24, no. 10 (August 21, 2013): 2125–27. doi.org/10.1177
/0956797613485603.

Csikszentmihalyi, Mihaly. *Flow: The Psychology of Optimal Experience.* New
York: Harper Perennial, 2008.

Diener, Ed, and Micaela Y. Chan. "Happy People Live Longer: Subjective
Well-Being Contributes to Health and Longevity." *Applied Psychology:
Health and Well-Being* 3, no. 1 (January 27, 2011): 1–43. doi.org/10.1111/j
.1758-0854.2010.01045.x.

Duckworth, Angela L., and Martin E.P. Seligman. "Self-Discipline Outdoes
IQ in Predicting Academic Performance of Adolescents." *Psychological
Science* 16, no. 12 (2005): 939–44. doi.org/10.1111/j.1467-9280.2005.01641.x.

Duval, Shelley, and Robert A. Wicklund. *A Theory of Objective Self-Awareness.*
Cambridge, MA: Academic Press, 1972.

Dweck, Carol S. *Mindset: The New Psychology of Success.* New York: Random
House, 2006.

Ellis, Albert. "The Revised ABC's of Rational-Emotive Therapy (RET)."
Journal of Rational-Emotive & Cognitive-Behavior Therapy 9, no. 3 (1991):
139–72. doi.org/10.1007/BF01061227.

Emmons, Robert A., and Michael E. McCullough. "Counting Blessings
Versus Burdens: An Experimental Investigation of Gratitude and
Subjective Well-Being in Daily Life." *Journal of Personality and Social
Psychology* 84, no. 2 (2003): 377–89. doi.org/10.1037/0022-3514.84.2.377.

Eurich, Tasha. "What Self-Awareness Really Is (and How to Cultivate It)."
    Harvard Business Review, January 4, 2018. hbr.org/2018/01/what-self
    -awareness-really-is-and-how-to-cultivate-it.

Gillebaart Marleen. "The 'Operational' Definition of Self-Control." *Frontiers
    in Psychology* 9 (July 2018): 1231. doi.org/10.3389/fpsyg.2018.01231.

Greater Good Science Center. "Mindfulness Defined." *Greater Good
    Magazine*. Accessed March 2, 2023. greatergood.berkeley.edu/topic
    /mindfulness/definition#how-cultivate-mindfulness.

Hampson, Sarah E., Grant W. Edmonds, Maureen Barckley, Lewis
    R. Goldberg, Joan P. Dubanoski, and Teresa A. Hillier. "A Big Five
    Approach to Self-Regulation: Personality Traits and Health Trajectories
    in the Hawaii Longitudinal Study of Personality and Health." *Psychology,
    Health & Medicine* 21, no. 2 (2016): 152–62. doi.org/10.1080/13548506
    .2015.1061676.

Hanson, Rick. "How to Change Your Brain." Greater Good Science Center.
    September 9, 2011. Video. youtube.com/watch?v=gDl6_9TmgCY&t=38s.

Isbel, Ben, Jan Weber, Jim Lagopoulos, Kayla Stefanidis, Hanna Anderson,
    and Matthew J. Summers. "Neural Changes in Early Visual Processing
    After 6 Months of Mindfulness Training in Older Adults." *Scientific
    Reports* 10, no. 21163 (2020). nature.com/articles/s41598-020-78343-w.

Kabat-Zinn, Jon. "Mindfulness-Based Interventions in Context: Past,
    Present, and Future." *Clinical Psychology: Science and Practice* 10, no. 2
    (2003): 144–56. doi.org/10.1093/clipsy.bpg016.

Katherine, Anne. *Boundaries: Where You End and I Begin*. Center City, MN:
    Hazelden Publishing, 2010.

Keng, Shian-Ling, Moria J. Smoski, and Clive J. Robins. "Effects of
    Mindfulness on Psychological Health: A Review of Empirical Studies."
    Clinical Psychology Review 31, no. 6 (August 2011): 1041–56. doi.org/10
    .1016/j.cpr.2011.04.006.

Kohli, Sonali. "Modern-Day Segregation in Public Schools." *The Atlantic*, November 18, 2014. theatlantic.com/education/archive/2014/11/modern -day-segregation-in-public-schools/382846/.

Lyubomirsky, Sonja. *The How of Happiness: A Scientific Approach to Getting the Life You Want*. New York: Penguin, 2007.

Lyubomirsky, Sonja, Laura King, and Ed Diener. "The Benefits of Frequent Positive Affect: Does Happiness Lead to Success?" *Psychological Bulletin* 131, no. 6 (2005): 803–55. apa.org/pubs/journals/releases/bul-1316803.pdf.

Martínez, Nicole, Cynthia D. Connelly, Alexa Pérez, and Patricia Calero. "Self-Care: A Concept Analysis." *International Journal of Nursing Sciences* 8, no. 4 (2021): 418–25. doi.org/10.1016/j.ijnss.2021.08.007.

Merton, Robert K. "The Self-Fulfilling Prophecy." *The Antioch Review* 8, no. 2 (1948): 193–210. doi.org/10.2307/4609267.

Mindful USC. "Mindfulness Myths." Accessed March 1, 2023. mindful.usc .edu/myths/.

Mindset Kit. "Do's & Don'ts of Praise." mindsetkit.org/topics/praise-process -not-person/dos-donts-of-praise.

Mischel, Walter, Ebbe B. Ebbesen, and Antonette Raskoff Zeiss. "Cognitive and Attentional Mechanisms in Delay of Gratification." *Journal of Personality and Social Psychology* 21, no. 2 (1972): 204–18. doi.org/10.1037 /h0032198.

Mueller, Claudia M., and Carol S. Dweck. "Praise for Intelligence Can Undermine Children's Motivation and Performance." *Journal of Personality and Social Psychology* 75, no. 1 (July 1998): 33–52. doi.org/10 .1037/0022-3514.75.1.33.

Nash, Jo. "How to Set Healthy Boundaries & Build Positive Relationships." Positive Psychology. January 5, 2018. positivepsychology.com/great-self -care-setting-healthy-boundaries/.

National Alliance of Mental Illness. "The Mental Health Benefits of Religion & Spirituality." *NAMI Blog.* December 21, 2016. nami.org/Blogs/NAMI -Blog/December-2016/The-Mental-Health-Benefits-of-Religion-Spiritual.

Neff, Kristen D. "The Role of Self-Compassion in Development: A Healthier Way to Relate to Oneself." *Human Development* 52, no. 4 (June 2009): 211–14. doi.org/10.1159/000215071.

Newman, Kira M. "Do Mindful People Have a Stronger Sense of Self?" *Greater Good Magazine*, March 14, 2017. greatergood.berkeley.edu/article /item/do_mindful_people_have_a_stronger_sense_of_self.

Ottenstein, Sybil. "3 Biggest Myths About Boundaries: And Why We Need Them." *The Now* (blog). *Psychology Today.* December 10, 2020. psychologytoday.com/us/blog/the-now/202012/3-biggest-myths-about -boundaries.

Padilla-Walker, Laura M., Madison K. Memmott-Elison, and Larry J. Nelson. "Positive Relationships as an Indicator of Flourishing During Emerging Adulthood." In *Flourishing in Emerging Adulthood: Positive Development During the Third Decade of Life.* Edited by Laura M. Padilla-Walker and Larry J. Nelson, 212–36. New York: Oxford University Press, 2017.

Perry, Elizabeth. "What Is Self-Awareness and How To Develop It." *Well-Being* (blog). BetterUp, August 20, 2019. betterup.com/blog/what-is-self -awareness.

Peterson, Christopher, and Lisa C. Barrett. "Explanatory Style and Academic Performance among University Freshman." *Journal of Personality and Social Psychology* 53, no. 3 (1987): 603–7. doi.org/10.1037/0022-3514.53.3.603.

Peterson, Christopher, and Martin E. P. Seligman. "Explanatory Style and Illness." *Journal of Personality* 55, no. 2 (1987): 237–65. psycnet.apa.org /record/1988-26552-001.

Pew Research Center. "Religion's Relationship to Happiness, Civic Engagement and Health Around the World." Pew Research Center. January 31, 2019. pewresearch.org/religion/2019/01/31/religions-relationship -to-happiness-civic-engagement-and-health-around-the-world/.

PsychCare Psychological Services. "Hardwired for Connection."
PsychCare. Accessed June 13, 2023. psychcaremd.com/hardwired
-for-connection/#:~:text=Humans%20are%20hardwired%20for
%20connection,re%20interacting%20with%20other%20people.

Rath, Tom, and Jim Harter. "The Five Essential Elements of Well-Being."
gallup.com. May 5, 2010. gallup.com/workplace/237020/five-essential
-elements.aspx.

Rath, Tom, and Jim Harter. *Wellbeing: The Five Essential Elements*. New York:
Gallup Press, 2010.

Schnitker, Sarah A., and Robert A. Emmons. "The Psychology of Virtue:
Integrating Positive Psychology and the Psychology of Religion."
Psychology of Religion and Spirituality 9, no. 3 (2017): 239–41. doi.org/10
.1037/rel0000133.

Seligman, Martin E.P. *Authentic Happiness: Using the New Positive Psychology
to Realize Your Potential for Lasting Fulfillment*. New York: Free Press, 2002.

Simon-Thomas, Emiliana R. "Meditation Makes Us Act with Compassion."
Greater Good Magazine, April 11, 2013. greatergood.berkeley.edu/article
/item/meditation_causes_compassionate_action.

Singh, Nirbhay N., Guilio E. Lanconi, Alan S. W. Winton, Judy Singh, W.
John Curtis, Robert G. Wahler, and Kristen M. McAleavey. "Mindful
Parenting Decreases Aggression and Increases Social Behavior in Children
with Developmental Disabilities." *Behavior Modification* 31,
no. 6 (November 2007): 749–71.

Strohecker, James. "What Is Wellness?" PDF, 2015. is.muni.cz/el/1451
/podzim2015/e031/um/TRAVIS_STROHECKER_What_is_Wellness.pdf.

Sze, Jocelyn A, Anett Gyurak, Joyce W. Yuan, and Robert W. Levenson.
"Coherence Between Emotional Experience and Physiology: Does Body
Awareness Training Have an Impact?" *Emotion* 10, no. 6 (2010): 803–14.
doi.org/10.1037/a0020146.

Tang, Yi-Yuan, Yinghua Ma, Junghon Wang, Yaxin Fan, Shigang Feng, Qilin Lu, Qingbao Yu, Danni Sui, and Mary K. Rothbart. "Short-Term Meditation Training Improves Attention and Self-Regulation." *Proceedings of the National Academy of Sciences* 104, no. 43 (October 23, 2007): 17152–56. doi.org/10.1073/pnas.0707678104.

Tawwab, Nedra Glover. *Set Boundaries, Find Peace: A Guide to Reclaiming Yourself.* New York: TarcherPerigee, 2021.

Umberson, Debra, and Jennifer Karas Montez. "Social Relationships and Health: A Flashpoint for Health Policy." *Journal of Health and Social Behavior* 51, no. 1 (October 8, 2010): 54–66. doi.org/10.1177/0022146510383501.

Wright, Stephanie A. "All About Rational Emotive Behavior Therapy (REBT)." PsychCentral.com. Updated April 15, 2022. psychcentral.com/lib/rational-emotive-behavior-therapy/.

Yilmaz, Eser. "Self-Fulfilling Prophecy: Definition, Examples, and Theories." Berkeley Well-Being Institute. August 25, 2021. berkeleywellbeing.com/self-fulfilling-prophecy.html.

Zetlin, Minda. "How Emotionally Intelligent People Use the 'Hell Yes' Rule to Achieve More in Less Time." *Inc.* October 29, 2022. inc.com/minda-zetlin/time-management-setting-priorities-dr-richard-shuster-work-life-balance.html.

ABOUT THE AUTHOR

Chianti Lomax is a sought-after international speaker, certified coach, corporate trainer and accomplished transformation strategist who thrives at the intersection of mindfulness, technology, and transformative coaching. As a certified personal and executive coach, workplace mindfulness facilitator, and positive psychology practitioner, Chianti believes in the power of bite-sized habit changes that help increase our well-being and elevate the overall human experience.

With sixteen years of experience in the tech transformation industry as an organizational change and adult-learning consultant, Chianti has also helped organizations transform their people, processes, and technology through human-centered training and coaching programs. With the ability to translate a mindset centered in transformational living to the Big Tech industry, Chianti's experience has provided a bridge between technology and mindfulness and between the Black female community and corporate and tech titans such as IBM, Accenture, and Deloitte Consulting.

In 2016, Chianti founded the Happy Pop-Up, an interactive wellness experience that makes positive psychology accessible to the everyday person through fun and engaging activities that feel like the ultimate adult playdate. In a post-pandemic world, Chianti plans to relaunch the pop-up as a vehicle to continue the conversation around mental agility and generational well-being for Black and brown communities around the world.

ABOUT SOUNDS TRUE

Sounds True was founded in 1985 by Tami Simon with a clear mission: to disseminate spiritual wisdom. Since starting out as a project with one woman and her tape recorder, we have grown into a multimedia publishing company with a catalog of more than 3,000 titles by some of the leading teachers and visionaries of our time, and an ever-expanding family of beloved customers from across the world.

In more than three decades of evolution, Sounds True has maintained our focus on our overriding purpose and mission: to wake up the world. We offer books, audio programs, online learning experiences, and in-person events to support your personal growth and awakening, and to unlock our greatest human capacities to love and serve.

At SoundsTrue.com you'll find a wealth of resources to enrich your journey, including our weekly *Insights at the Edge* podcast, free downloads, and information about our nonprofit Sounds True Foundation, where we strive to remove financial barriers to the materials we publish through scholarships and donations worldwide.

To learn more, please visit SoundsTrue.com/freegifts or call us toll-free at 800.333.9185.

Together, we can wake up the world.

sounds true
WAKING UP THE WORLD